O dammit!

William Cowper Brann, 1895, courtesy of The Texas Collection, Baylor University, Waco.

O dammit!

A Lexicon and Lecture
from
William Cowper Brann, The Iconoclast

Jerry Flemmons

Texas Tech University Press

This book was set in New 702BT and Prestige. The paper used in this book meets the minimum requirements of ANSI/NISO Z39.48-1992 (R1997).♾

Design by Melissa Bartz

Printed in the United States of America

Library of Congress Cataloging-in-Publication Data
O dammit! : a lexicon and lecture from William Cowper Brann, the iconoclast / [compiled by] Jerry Flemmons.
p. cm.
Contents: O dammit! : being a lexicon of venom, vitriol, and vigorous witticisms / from William Cowper Brann and The iconoclast—O dammit! : an evening with The iconoclast.
ISBN 0-89672-405-0 (alk. paper)
1. Brann, William Cowper, 1855-1898—Quotations. 2. Brann, William Cowper, 1855-1898—Drama. 3. Authors, American—19th century—Drama. 4. Journalists—United States—Drama. 5. Quotations, American. I. Flemmons, Jerry. II. Brann, William Cowper, 1855-1898. Selections. 1998. III. Flemmons, Jerry. O dammit!
PS1121.B53A6 1898
818'.409—dc21 98-24591
CIP

98 99 00 01 02 03 04 05 06 / 9 8 7 6 5 4 3 2 1

Texas Tech University Press
Box 41037
Lubbock, Texas 79409-1037 USA

800-832-4042

ttup@ttu.edu
Http://www.ttup.ttu.edu

For all practicing William Brann iconoclastic apostles
everywhere
. . . And those few old historian Baptist soreheads
Who can neither forgive nor forget

Kind Reader, have a care!
For aught I know this . . . may be the rankest literature, and reading it may wreck your immortal soul . . . granting of course that you are in possession of such perishable property.

. . . .

Don't imagine for one moment this paper is published expressly to please you.

—William Cowper Brann, 1855-1898

Introduction

I first met William Brann in college where he was held up as a kind of marauding journalist knight-errant cleansing the late nineteenth century of hypocrisy and moral treachery. Sophomore journalism students will believe almost anything. Years later, two decades ago, I found him again in a used bookstore, stacked haphazardly on a dark, top shelf, dusty and covered by spiderwebs and neglect. He and his writings were there in twelve volumes, which the shop clerk was pleased to sell me for seventy-five dollars, a bargain for the collected works of a man critics once considered the H. L. Mencken of his era and an original American writer.

I read the twelve volumes, taking notes as I went, thinking, perhaps, to deliver Brann from obscurity with a biography, but through an adult's eyes I saw a complex man, a brilliant writer but one whose whole life encompassed an almost Faustian inventory of weaknesses and strengths and whose story resonated with all the triumph and tragedy of a Homeric epic. William Cowper Brann was all too human. Ordinary biography seemed inadequate.

The answer was to allow Brann to tell his own story, in his own words, and *O dammit!* came into being. I think of this one-man stage play as a lecture because Brann spoke in theaters and public halls across Texas and the South. Audiences came to hear the eloquence of a man who had conquered the English language, who declaimed with a crusader's zealotry and passion, and stalked stages with an actor's theatricality. He gave his audiences laughter and tears and a broad humanity. Viewed across the expanse of a century, his ideas seem almost contemporary.

O dammit! was first presented as a reading, part of a new playwright's series sponsored by Southern Methodist University, then debuted on a Texas A&M University at Commerce stage. It went on for more than a hundred performances in Texas and as far away as Washington, D.C.

The lecture does not tell it all, and there were leftover notes. The iconoclast had more to say and I went back through the twelve volumes, withdrawing additional ideas and writings, arranging them under various subjects. These became *O dammit!* the lexicon, in which Brann comments on everything from high society to God to Prohibition to cats to the English to missionaries to love and the universe . . .

. . . and Baptists, to be sure, always the Baptists.

He and they were together throughout *The Iconoclast*'s existence, even on the final day.

William Cowper Brann's life ended April 1, 1898, late afternoon on a busy downtown Waco, Texas, street, shot in the back, the bullet entering at the precise point at which his suspenders crossed. Brann returned fire and mortally wounded his assassin, businessman Tom Davis. Both men died within a few hours. Brann's funeral and burial in Oakwood Cemetery attracted Waco's largest crowd in history, although many came as spectators, not mourners, and, it was said, only to ensure that the hated Iconoclast and Apostle of the Devil indeed was dead and at long last in Hell.

Assassination is the absolute censorship of a writer, but there were those in Waco who felt Brann's death was not severe enough punishment for what they considered his gravest sin: heretical slander and libel of the town's Baptists and their denominational training center, Baylor University, which he termed "that little museum of mental misfits."

Admirers outside Waco eulogized Brann as a "Prairie Voltaire," the "American Carlyle," a literary and intellectual giant of the nineteenth century and analog to Shakespeare and Milton, Pope and Byron, Swift and Goethe—lofty company for a man with scant formal education, one who had lived and worked in extreme poverty and anonymity as a newspaper writer and editor for most of his forty-three years.

William Brann became famous, and infamous, and dead, in only forty months as author, editor, and publisher of *The Iconoclast,* a small magazine which spread with success throughout America and into at least a dozen foreign countries, ultimately achieving a circulation of perhaps 120,000. He boasted of a one million monthly readership, a remarkable figure for the era, if true, and astonishing for a nineteenth-century publication issued out of "stale, flat, and literarily unprofitable" Waco, or, as Brann was fond of calling his adopted hometown: "Wack-o."

Brann lured readers to *The Iconoclast* with a thunderous, passionate prose style and ideological bombast, a genius grasp of descriptive language and a searing slash-and-burn wit that feared no idiom, issue, or ism. He was the complete eclectic writer, the embodiment of a classic iconoclast which, the dictionary tells us, is "one who attacks established beliefs, ideals, customs, or institutions." That explains why Brann, who could write, "The Bible tells us that God made a perfect man and let him degenerate until he began to breed Baptists," was unpopular in Waco.

Brann was a consequential literary figure in America yet is virtually forgotten today except by a few scholars and budding authors who seek out his substantial body of writings—collected essays from *The Iconoclast's* forty-month life total more than a million words and thirty-six hundred pages in twelve volumes. Brann's words reveal a wise, literate, erudite, earthy, often angry and contradictory, highly complex personality, a man of grand, although sometimes shrill, petty, unreasonable, and intemperate passions, in tenacious, almost obsessive, pursuit of what he considered The Truth. His style and attitudes, and his prejudices, were very much of his time and place but widely ranged from Shakespearean grandiloquent to self-deprecating, self-assured to self-doubt, mannered to crude, bright optimism to misanthropic despair ("There's still more shadow than sunshine, less pleasure than pain . . ."). His biographer, Charles Carver, described Brann as a "ringmaster of phrases who could flick his pen and blend editorial force, an immense vocabulary, and a ribald streak into a monthly circus. The acts changed as smoothly as the turning of the pages, and the band was wistful, militant, or raucous, depending on the mood of the master. There was enough Bach and Beethoven. . . . to draw the sophisticates, enough bump-and-grind burlesque to ensure stamping in the gallery. And what gave Brann's circus a fascinating Lewis Carroll touch was the frequent incongruous juxtaposition of the two."

To experience Brann's absolute robust power ("colossal, crude, terrible, and sublime"), one must go to the original source, those now-dusty essays in which he seizes the scruff of an idea and flails it about the printed page in a maelstrom of metaphor and alliteration, simile and slang, classical allusion and figurative poetical idiom, perverted, inverted, often invented-on-the-fly phrase and adjective, archaic malediction and Texas cussing—all imploded within epic sentences yoked like matched thoroughbreds with pounds of commas and semicolons, ampersands, virgules, jim dashes and exclamation points. When William Brann wanted to say something, he said it every way he could.

Brann was one part consummate essayist, one part cracker-barrel philosopher, one part religious disciple (ruefully, he termed himself "apostle" and "preacher" and his *Iconoclast* "the great Religious Monthly," to the consternation of real clergymen who railed against him from America's fundamental pulpits), and one part anti-tradition heretic, a splendid though often ambivalent human alloy of cow lot Don Quixote and Oxford Don lecturing on mankind's foibles and frailties as he perceived them.

It was his use of language—a pungent, eye-arching vaudeville of English—that set Brann apart from ordinary writers. To Brann, Grover Cleveland was "His Gutosity," a "pointy-headed" politician who ran on the "Middle-of-the-Muck" ticket to become an "anthropological curio Oofty-Gofty." Brann called a group of editors "a lobeliaceous aggregation of lollipops." America's society crowd was composed of "dudes" and "dudines," rural areas were "Gooberdom" and small towns "Jayville." Journalism was "highfalutin' flubdub" and love could be the "goo-a-roo" and "ootsie-wootsie."

Dogmatic clergymen especially were butts of Brann's venomous "whip of scorpions." "Atribilarius" preachers were "sanctimonious slang-slingers," religious "whangdoodles" and "hoo-doos," "sweet-scented slugs of sanctified slobber," "rotten-hearted thimble-riggers," "pulpit-thrumming gowkthrapples," "blabsters," "bubblyjocks," and a "brace of Pecksnifflian curs" who "peddle hallelujahs at two dollars apiece."

Fundamentalist preachers appreciated little of Brann's caustic wit—one historian called him a mean Mark Twain—and boycotted sale of *The Iconoclast* wherever they could. He was not an atheist as they alleged, only a deist in the tradition of Jefferson and Paine, but for hard-core Baptist Waco any theological detour was godless, hellish, and there were those who sincerely believed Brann was sent by the devil as a plague on the town.

Waco of the 1890s was a peculiar place for an iconoclast to practice. Deeply religious, dominated by the Baptists, there were four major theological colleges, including Baylor. Waco, however, was still a town on the Texas frontier, sometimes known as Six-Shooter Depot, with a licensed red-light district called The Reservation, open saloons, gambling, and frequent gunfights. Preachers there never lacked for sermon topics.

William Brann arrived in Waco in 1894 for the same reason he frequently went to other towns. He needed work. Most of his adult life he had been an itinerant newspaper man, an unlikely profession for a man born into the rural 1855 poverty of Humboldt Township, Coles County, Illinois. Brann's mother died when he was two and his father, a country minister, gave him to a farmer, William Hawkins. At age thirteen, he ran away and never returned, supporting himself as a hotel bellboy in Saint Louis. Later, he pitched on a semiprofessional baseball team, managed an opera company, was a railroad brakeman, and finally a newspaperman.

He came to Texas to work on newspapers in Galveston, then he moved to the *Houston Post,* to Austin, to San Antonio, back to Austin and, ultimately, Waco. During his first stint in Austin, Brann tried publishing *The Texas Iconoclast* but the paper never found an audience and he sold it to a fellow writer, William Sidney Porter, who also failed (Porter later changed his name to O. Henry and became a short story immortal). In Waco, Brann revived *The Iconoclast* and found instant, spectacular success.

By mid-1897, Brann was revered nationally and detested by Waco fundamentalists. Antonia Teixeira had arrived in Waco. She was about eleven, Brazilian, sent to Baylor for an education and training as a missionary. Instead, she became a kitchen maid in the home of Rufus Burleson, Baylor's president, and, after two years, she became pregnant. Antonia claimed she had been raped by Steen Morris, the brother of the son-in-law of Dr. Burleson. William Brann sharpened his stub-pencil and went after the Baptists with blazing words. Antonia gave birth prematurely. The baby, which Brann called "a pretty, two-pound Baylor diploma," died. Morris was indicted, brought to trial, and acquitted when Antonia changed her earlier story (Brann intimated that the girl had been bribed). She left Waco and disappeared from history, but the town was divided by the controversy and Brann began carrying a pistol. In November 1897, a friend and vocal supporter of Brann's position on Baylor, Judge G. B. Gerald, fought a gun battle with the Harris brothers, local newspaper publishers, on a downtown street. The brothers were killed and Gerald so badly wounded that he lost an arm.

Brann was attacked twice. First by Baylor students who came to his office, dragged him to the campus, and threatened to hang him from the oak tree which still stands in front of the university's old administration building. Probably the student mob meant only to frighten him, but he escaped after faculty members intervened. Later a group of men, led by a member of Baylor's board of managers, horsewhipped Brann outside *The Iconoclast* office. Then Tom Davis darted from a late afternoon crowd on that stormy April afternoon and shot William Brann in the back.

Friends tried to keep *The Iconoclast* going, but without Brann's unique literary style, the paper failed after one issue. Admirers predicted that William Brann's words and wisdom would live forever, yet he and his work were gone from memories all too quickly.

Perhaps William Brann was little more than a clever pamphleteer, just a gifted newspaper man—in his words, a "two-dollar skyrocket on a dark night," but the man had something to say, and what he said, how he said it, is as entertaining as ever.

O dammit!

Being a Lexicon of Venom, Vitriol, and Vigorous Witticisms

From
William Cowper Brann
and *The Iconoclast*

Prologue

The Iconoclast Speaks

Ladies and Gentlemen: There are many things which I cordially dislike, but my pet aversion is what is known as a "set" lecture—one of those stereotyped affairs ground out with studied inflection and practiced gesture; hence, I shall ask permission to talk to you as informally and as freely as though we were seated in friendly converse around the soda fount of a Kansas City drug store, and I want you to feel free to talk back as though we had gotten into this difficulty by accident instead of design. With such unbounded liberty there's really no telling whither we shall drift, what subjects we may touch upon. But should I inadvertently trample upon any of your social idols or political gods, I trust that you will take no offense—will remember that we may honestly differ, that none of us are altogether infallible. Lest any of you mistake me for an oratorical clearing-sale or elocutionary bargain-counter, expect a Demosthenic display and be disappointed, I hasten to say that I am no orator as Brutus was, but simply a plain, blunt man, like Mark [*sic*] Antony, who spoke right on and said what he did know, or thought he knew, which was just as satisfactory to himself. He's dead now, poor fellow. Woman in the case, of course....

• • • • •

The Iconoclast [does not exist] with the expectation that it will reform the world—will drag the Golden Age in by the ears or pull the millennium before it is ripe. If it does but succeed in exposing a few Frauds and peeling the cuticle from an occasional Fake—if it can but recover a few square acres of Mother Earth from the domain of Falsehood and Folly, from the dominion of Darkness and the Devil, it will not have lived and labored in vain.

O dammit!

For years I have heard the cry that the world needs builders, not iconoclasts, and it has invariably come from those who have builded nothing, who don't know the difference between an assault on things sacred and an antidote for the itch, who object to having humbugs exposed lest they find their own breeches at half-mast in a Dakota blizzard.

• • • • •

It is the iconoclasts who break down political prescription and religious praemunire and thereby make improvement possible. Such men make grievous blunders; all men of action do. They are seldom wise. . . .

• • • • •

I have believed many things with all my soul only to find them false.

• • • • •

I prefer those who believe too much to those who believe too little.

• • • • •

It is very fortunate that I am the last of the Apostles instead of the first of the Deities.

• • • • •

I am the apostle of the white-winged Goddess of Peace. I always carry a cruse of oil in my hip-pocket to cast upon the troubled waters. I have a pacific effect on all with whom I come in contact. Children quit crying when they see me coming, women speak well of their neighbors, men respect each other's political opinions, preachers engage in silent prayer, and the lion and the lamb lie down together.

• • • • •

Perhaps it is unnecessary to state that I'm not posing as a saint. I may eventually become an angel—of some sort—but I'll wear no wings.

• • • • •

I paint man as I find him, not as I would have him. I did not create him, nor did his Architect ask my advice; hence, it is no fault of mine that his virtue's frail as ocean foam—not mine the blame that while half a god he's all a beast.

• • • • •

I am, sir, an "avowed champion" of every religion that has pierced Life's Dark Shadows with one ray of sunshine. I am an "avowed champion" of every American citizen whose civic rights are invaded because of his religious convictions.

• • • • •

This is Sunday morning, and it is safe to say that while I pen this paragraph more than a hundred preachers are pounding away at *The Iconoclast* in their pulpits—thereby causing all the curious sisters to resolve to read it secretly. I sometimes wonder if God didn't raise those fellows up especially to act as my agents—to indirectly aid me in imbuing the whole world with the idea that every religion which makes people better and happier is really worth reverence.

• • • • •

The Iconoclast, like the other mills of God, grinds slowly, but it grinds exceedingly small.

A

America

It is but a new thing—a great straddling political calf standing doubtfully upon its four wobbly legs, the bones of which still but gristle, the tendons mere fatty strings. Thus it stands, fronting time, foolishly imagining itself a winged-lion or hippogriff. If it meet with no mishap until its bones have time to harden—until its principles still in a nebulous state are finally fixed—it will doubtless become, if not an immortal winged-creature, at least a fine horned-bull, able to paw the dirt and bellow with the proudest of bovines . . . but infant governments, like juveniles, have their perils to pass through, their colics and cramps, measles and mumps, and it is a long cry from the baptismal font to the *toga virilis*—from wobbly foolish calfhood to mastership of the world.

• • • • •

Forty old separate and distinct buildings of different styles of architecture huddled together helter-skelter under one rickety patchwork roof, hovering aloft with painful effort, pulled at, even shot at, the props all rotten and worm-eaten—the fact scarce concealed by liberal paint and cheap gilding.

Americans

The American can do nothing with moderation.

• • • • •

Life with the American people is one continental hurry and rush from the cradle to the grave. We're born in a hurry, live by electricity, and die with scientific expedition. Half of us don't take time to become acquainted with our own families. We've even got to courting by telephone, and I expect to see some enterprising firm put up lovers' kisses in tablet form, so that they can be carried in the vest pocket and absorbed while we figure cent per cent, or make out a mortgage.

• • • • •

The Norse Viking no longer plows the unknown wave, his heart wilder than the wat'ry waste, his arm stronger than tempered steel; he comes to America and starts a saloon.

The American Flag

The American flag, like the American female, should not flaunt itself in public until it becomes an eyesore.

• • • • •

A flag that is good enough to live under is good enough to fight for.

Anglo-Saxons

The Saxons were a low German tribe that dwelt at and near the mouth of the Elbe about 1,600 years ago. How they happened to get there nobody knows, but from the coldness of their blood and the sluggishness of their brain I opine that they evoluted from the oyster.

The Associated Press

. . . that busy collector of compost.

• • • • •

The most grasping news agency, the most impudent news agency, and the most incompetent news agency in the history of the world is . . . The Associated Press. When you see a newspaper man working for it you need look for no further proof that he is unable to hold a job anywhere else.

O dammit!

Atheism

Why play at atheism because others have failed to describe the indescribable, to comprehend the incomprehensible and make it plain to men of little minds? Do we seek the incense of a rose with a microscope, or the taste of a truffle with hay scales? Can you take the cube root of the mock-bird's trill or handle the rainbow with a pair of ice tongs?

Atheists

The church should recognize the fact that no man is an atheist by choice.

• • • • •

Atheists deny the existence of God because He doesn't move in their set.

• • • • •

To make them understand a message, God would have to typewrite it, add the seal of a notary public, and deliver it in person.

• • • • •

In denying God, he denies the efficient cause of his own moral concept, of his own civilization; but to disclaim a cause does not abrogate its effect. Denial of the law of gravitation from now until doomsday will not cause water to run up hill instead of down.

• • • • •

An atheist once solemnly assured me that he couldn't possibly believe anything he couldn't prove, but when I asked him what led him to take such a lively interest in the welfare of his wife's children, became almost as angry as a Calvinist whose Confession of Faith had been called in question.

B

Babies

All babies look much alike, whether born heir to millions or to a ragpicker's route—little blear-eyed balls somewhat resembling a raw beefsteak.

Bachelorhood

Adam was at one time a bachelor, therefore his own boss.

Barbers

The barber who will learn to breathe through his ears need never want for a job.

Baptists

The Bible tells us that God made a perfect man and let him degenerate until he began to breed Baptists.

• • • • •

They constitute the grandest aggregation of ignorance, bigotry, and bile on which God's sun ever shone.

• • • • •

A Baptist don't want to think; he just wants to believe—and take a bath. If he should think he couldn't believe, and if he didn't believe he'd be damned.

• • • • •

The Baptists have never proclaimed or practiced religious liberty when they possessed the power to persecute.

O dammit!

• • • • •

No human soul can break into Heaven via the Baptist gate without first securing the consent of "the pastor or deacons," who are supposed to carry the keys of the Kingdom of God in their pants! And the devil wunk the other eye.

• • • • •

The Baptist church always has a number of highly interesting heretic hunts on hand. It is forever getting into trouble through ministers who imagine that their heads were made for thought as well as the emission of sound. Its patience is sorely tried by these contumacious preachers. I suggest that it protect itself by having the heads of all candidates for Baptist pulpits examined by the aid of X-Ray. The presence of a spoonful of gray matter, or the slightest suspicion of mental activity, should exclude the candidate.

• • • • •

Deny Christ, insult the Virgin, and blaspheme the name of God, and they'll forgive you, but insinuate that their little ticky-tailed preachers are a set of blatant asses who ought to braid their ears, and they'll boycott you simply because they dare not crucify.

• • • • •

The more ignorant an animal is, the more bigoted Baptist it is likely to be. I cannot at present think of a single American of distinction who was a member of that denomination. I have passed in mental review the great American statesmen, soldiers, authors, and inventors, and find only one among them who was web-footed. [President James A.] Garfield was a Cambellite—and had he not been murdered no one would have suspected he was a great man.

• • • • •

Doubtless there are many good people who are Baptists but God's sunlight never fell upon one who was not a bigot.

• • • • •

The Baptist church breeds bigotry just as a dead mule does maggots.

• • • • •

One cannot write philosophic essays while dallying with the Baptist faith. It were too much like mixing Websterian dignity with a cataleptiod convulsion, or sitting on a red ant hill and trying to look unconcerned.

• • • • •

I'll wager a scholarship at Baylor University that there are not in the entire Baptist ministry 100 men—not hydrocephalic—whose heads will fill a No. 7 hat.

• • • • •

The dreadful scandal at Baylor University suggests that we do not hold our Baptists under water long enough.

Baylor

. . . little museum of mental misfits.

• • • • •

Waco is becoming a famous watering place. She has the finest bathhouse in the world, a Baptist university.

• • • • •

The Iconoclast desires to see Baylor a veritable pantechnicon of learning—at least a place where the careful student may acquire something really worth remembering—instead of a Squeeritic graft to relieve simple Baptist folk of their hard-earned boodle by beludaling the brains of their bairns with miscalled education.

• • • • •

Time was when the faculty of Baylor was the pride of the state. Those were the days when many of the noblest men and women of Texas were educated within its walls. They love their Alma Mater, not for what she is, but for what she was. The old professors are gone, have been supplanted in great part by a lot of priorient little preachers, selected by a board of trustees, half of whom couldn't tell a Greek root from a rutabaga, *Pons asinorum* from Balaam's ass.

• • • • •

I am informed that there has never been a time when the salary of the president of Baylor University exceeded $2,000 per annum—about half that of a good whiskey salesman.

• • • • •

Change is the order of the Universe, and as Baylor cannot very well become worse it must of necessity become better. It will have the unswerving support of *The Iconoclast*. I am even willing to conduct a night school free of charge for the instruction of its faculty if each member thereof will give bond not to seek a better paying situation elsewhere as soon as he learns something.

• • • • •

I noticed in one of the local papers that "Dallas wants Baylor," $50,000 to $75,000 worth. Doubtless I'm a hopeless heretic, but I don't believe a d——n word of it. Dallas doesn't want Baylor even a little bit. There isn't a town in this world that wants it except Waco. It is simply another Frankenstein monster that has destroyed its architect. Baylor spends no money here worth mentioning. Its students are chiefly forks-of-the-road yaps who curry horses or run errands for their board and wear the same underwear the year round. They take but two baths during their lifetime—one when they are born, the other when they are baptized. The institution is worth less than nothing to any town. It is the alma mater of mob violence. It is a chronic breeder of bigotry and bile. As a small Waco property owner, I will give it $1,000 any time to move to Dallas, and double that amount if it will go to Honolulu or Hell.

Bicycles & Women

The Women's Rescue League met recently at Washington and launched a double-shotted anathema at the female bike fiend. The Leaguers attribute to the bicycle craze "the alarming increase" in the number of courtesans, and call upon ministers and respectable women everywhere to denounce cycling by the sex as "vulgar and indecent." Doubtless the Rescuers imagine they have made a new discovery of inestimable benefit to society—have laid the ax to the root of that evil of which the bawdy-house is the flower and Hell the fruitage. Is the bike transforming this staid old world into one wild bacchic orgy or phallic revel? Have we toiled afoot thus far up the social mountainside, only to go bowling down on a pneumatic tire? Head us, somebody! Police!

• • • • •

I opine that the bike is a harmless instrument when properly handled. The trouble is not so much with the evasive machine as with the woman who straddles it. It will carry its rider to church as rapidly as to the Reservation [Waco's legalized prostitution district]. The bike is no more an incentive to bawdry than is a wheelbarrow. It doesn't make a woman depraved; it only renders her ridiculous.

The Bible

The Bible may be said to begin with a homicide and end with a holocaust.

• • • • •

The Bible is an anthology of ancient literature—a wonderful symposium of poetry and philosophy, the fierce love and fiercer hate, the wild worship and wilder waps of the old world.

• • • • •

The Bible is a great gold mine, in which inexhaustible store of yellow metal is mixed with much worthless rubbish that must be purged away by honest criticism before the book becomes really profitable—even fit for general circulation. I would rather place in the hands of an innocent girl a copy of the *Police Gazette* or [*New York*] *Sunday Sun* than an unexpurgated Bible. It is a book I value much, yet keep under lock and key with *Don Juan* and the *Decameron*. It contains both the grandest morality and most degrading obscenity every conceived in the brain of mortal man. There are passages whose beauty and power might cause the heart of an angel to leap in ecstasy, others that would call a blush of shame to the brassy front of the foulest fiend that ever howled and shrieked through the sulfurous valleys of Hell.

O dammit!

• • • • •

It is idle to urge that man should believe the Bible, for man should believe nothing, man can believe nothing, but what receives the sanction of his reason.

• • • • •

There are great truths in the Bible. It matters not to me whether they were revealed to Hebrew prophets in delirious trans-vision or borrowed of gentile philosophers who painfully worked them out by long years of study. There they are, with the stamp of God on them. Deep pools of wisdom there in that strange old book. Beautiful things there are, too, sometimes appearing as restful valleys amid the awful grandeur of thunder.

• • • • •

The Bible did not create man's belief in God's existence and his own immortality, but of this belief, old as Zoroaster, antedating Babylon, was the Bible born. It is simply an outward evidence of man's inward grace. I do accept the testimony of the Bible, but only as one of a crowd of witnesses. In questions of such grave import, we cannot have too much evidence; hence, it is strange indeed that anyone should make the Bible the sole foundation of his faith, should take his stand upon an infinitesimal portion of what the world knew in ages past. The Bible is but one of many sacred books in which man has borne witness that he is the favored creature of an Almighty Being, but one voice in a multitude singing hosannas to the Most High, a single note in the mighty diapason of the Universe.

• • • • •

The Bible assures us there is a God, science fails to demonstrate that there isn't—and there you are!

Books

If a book is only bad enough it is sure of popular success.

Business

The artist paints, the publisher prints, and the manager stages, not what the public should approve, but what it will pay for.

• • • • •

A banker is simply a man who buys and sells money, much as another trades in mules.

• • • • •

One may be a great lawyer or doctor, scientist or statesman, and at the same time a pauper; but he cannot be eminently successful in commerce and remain poor.

C

• • • • • • • • • • • • • • • •

Canada

Canada is but half civilized. It is still "loil" to old England, the strumpet of nations, the governmental harlot of history. It is to the Queen's apron strings like an idiot's scalp to the belt of an Apache squaw. Whenever John Bull whistles, it comes a-running like a half-grown spaniel at the call of a stableboy. It is the red bandanna upon which Britannia blows her protrusive bugle. It is the cuspidor into which she voids her royal rheum.

Capital Punishment

As matters now stand, one might slay a fellow mortal every year and stand an excellent chance of dying of old age, so far as the courts are concerned.

• • • • •

The man to be hanged for homicide usually repents and is jerked to Jesus, while his victim, cut off in the heyday of his sins, is supposed to go to Hell a-whopping.

The Cat

The cat is perhaps the only thing, with the exceptions of a bunion and a persistent creditor, that an unfortunate man can't manage to lose.

Catholicism

We have in this country a large contingent of ignorant fanatics who really believe that the Roman Catholic church is intent on overturning the American government and supplanting the President with the Pope, who are quite sure that the priesthood is a colossal aggregation of rogues and the convents but cloaks for all manner of immorality. The fact that the Pope has frequently expressed his admiration for the American government, that the Catholics were among the first to establish religious liberty in the western world, counts for nothing with these narrow-minded bigots, these hate-inflamed fanatics.

• • • • •

There are probably bad priests and unchaste nuns. With some hundreds of Protestant preachers in our penitentiaries—and as many of their female parishioners branded as bawds—it were indeed remarkable if all priests were paragons of purity.

Charity

The supreme test of a charitable mind is toleration for the opinions of others—an admission that perchance we do not know it quite all.

• • • • •

Too many people give to the poor only because it's "lending to the Lord"—and they expect Standard Oil dividends.

• • • • •

You may yawp in your $3,500 pulpit until ice forms in Perdition, you may sing Psalms until the cows come home, and agonize in prayer until your collar limps and you break a lung; you may visit all the sisters once a week and paddle about in the baptismal tank until you develop dorsal fins and web feet; you may believe the Bible from Alpha to Omega and the Baptist credo from A to Izzard; but if you have not Charity in the heart, you are no more than a cracked cymbal at a ten-cent circus.

Children

There is danger that our children will become so smart that we will not be able to understand them when they talk back, although they will always be able, by means of signs, to let us know the amount of cash they require.

Christianity

Christianity does not contain a single original idea. It borrowed liberally on every hand, but chiefly of Parseeism in which faith, as taught by Zoroaster—Aristotle says six thousand years before Plato—may be found its most important feature. It owes absolutely nothing to Judaism but the name of its God and an idle string of misinterpreted prophecies; is, from first to last, essentially a "Gentile" faith.

• • • • •

Christianity is optimism, not pessimism. It is a religion of joy instead of sorrow, of laughter rather than tears, of light and life, not of gloom and death.

• • • • •

The Christian religion is true or it is false. It is of God or it is of the Devil. If true it will stand the severest test. If of God it is indestructible as the law of gravitation.

Christians

Millions of tenderhearted people remain away from church simply because they cannot bear to witness the chronic gloom of those who have made their peace with God—the unhappiness of those poor creatures who are doomed to inherit an orthodox heaven.

• • • • •

I wouldn't preach five minutes to a man who looked as though his religion was hurting him—who seemed sorry he was going to be saved.

• • • • •

I have noticed that those who were most fearful that I would commit the awful sin of blasphemy, or "desecrate the Christian Sabbath" by playing ball with the boys or dancing with the girls were the people I had to watch closest in a trade; that those who sat up nights to agonize lest the young be led astray by some awful atheist, could tell the smoothest falsehood with the straightest face; that those who wept the most copiously because the heathen of foreign land had no Bible, were a trifle backward in supplying the heathen right here at home with bread.

Christmas

I never ate but one Christmas dinner for which I did not feel like apologizing to my doctor, and that was not eaten in strictly religious company. It was a regular Bohemian lunch partaken of on a Pullman by myself, a newspaper man, and two other sinners. We had tongue sandwiches and Budweiser, deviled ham and more beer. I remarked that we were awfully wicked, but the newspaper man consoled me by saying that Christ was something of a Bohemian himself.

The Church

Remember that "God is Everywhere"—even in church.

• • • • •

The working people are the first to espouse a religion and the last to relinquish. A theological tree dies first at the top—the spirit of indifference, of denial, develops earliest among the well-to-do. A church, in so far as the spirit of worship is concerned, is dead when it exists simply as an annex to polite society or commercial organization. A church cannot long exist without the hearty approval of the great middle class—those who earn bread in the sweat of the brow; for both the very rich and the very poor are, as a rule, not only irreligious, but vicious.

• • • • •

The church is not content with public supervision of the citizen; it follows him into his home and regulates his private habits, dictates what he shall eat and drink — sits at the muzzle to see how he loads himself.

President Grover Cleveland

. . . that old tub of guts and gall . . . a man more skilled in pinochle than diplomacy, who runs to belly rather than brains and drinks bourbon as if it were Weiss beer.

• • • • •

When Cleveland was reported assassinated the people naturally supposed he had been struck with an idea.

• • • • •

Cleveland is a "strong man" exactly as the hog is a strong animal. Stubborn without courage, persevering without judgment, and greedy without gratitude; these unpleasant characteristics Cleveland and the hog have in common. There are several other points of resemblance, but I have no desire to be hard on the hog.

• • • • •

Even the coming into the world of the Immaculate Son of God was not at the time considered nearly so important as the birth of Cleveland's last baby. But then His Father was not in politics.

• • • • •

The daily press announces that there is to be another Cleveland baby. It is to make its debut sometime this month. "Mrs. Cleveland has been sewing dainty garments all summer." Same old gush, gush, gush! slop, slop, slop! that has set the nation retching three times already. Good Lord! Will it never end. The fecundity of that family is becoming an American nightmare.

Cold Feet

Cold hands indicate a warm heart, but cold feet signify that there's going to be trouble in the family. Half the domestic infelicity and resultant divorces might be avoided were bridegrooms-elect permitted to take the temperatures of their fiancées' feet.

Conservatives

The apostle of *laissez-faire,* the boasted conservative—who is bond slave of custom and bows the knee to precedent—never accomplished anything of value in this world; never. He is simply a machine for the consumption of victuals, a rack upon which to hang old clothes.

The Cow

A muley cow will eat anything on this majestic earth that she can steal, from a hickory shirt to a Prohibition newspaper, and if she can't get it through her neck she will chew it and suck the juice. That's human nature to a hair.

D

The Dallas News

The Old Lady is a malevolent hypocrite, a journalistic harlot.

• • • • •

I do not know what others may think of this; but if I owned a dog degraded enough to utilize a copy of *The Dallas News* as a urinal I'd shoot him.

Dancing

Reverend J. H. Sims is loose in Kansas, and when last located was telling the Topekaites that "dancing destroys Christianity"; that it is "disgraceful and carnal . . . the absolute and certain route to hell." He tells what terrible things he would do should he find a man dancing with his wife. He is acquainted with the lady and I am not, but I suspect that the innuendo is undeserved. If he really believes, however, that she is of such fictile morals that she could not be trusted to go through the mazes of the waltz without falling from grace, he is certainly justified in keeping her under lock and key; but he has no right to judge the wives of others by public estimate of his own.

The Democratic Party

In the Democratic Party—which much resembles its political sister—we have high and low tariffites and free traders, gold-bugs, greenbackers, and bimetallists, all huddled together like household goods and barnyard refuse in the wake of a Kansas cyclone. It is simply a disorganized mob of political odds-and-ends such as Peter the Hermit led into Palestine.

The Devil

Too many people forget that while the Lord made the world, the Devil has been busy ever since putting on the finishing touches. I confess a sneaking respect for Satan, for he's preeminently a success in his chosen profession. He sat in on the game with a cash capital of one snake, and now he's got half the globe grabbed and an option on the other half.

Charles Dickens

As a manufacturer of fiction intended to kill time that might be better employed, Dickens stood at the head of his profession, and such honor as may be contained in this fact I accord him as freely as I would praise a trained pig or a ballet dancer. A man of genius may write an entertaining novel, just as a skilled jeweler may hammer out a horseshoe; but never did a man of superior intellect follow novel-grinding as a profession.

Dignity & Pride

When love fails and hope flies, pride still lingers, the savage rearguard of a human soul, and dies in the last ditch.

• • • • •

We realize that we don't amount to much and are ever fearful that our fellows will find it out. Hence, we buy $100 overcoats and go without undershirts, put costly plumes in our hats when there are holes in our only pair of stockings.

• • • • •

When I see a little man strut forth in the face of heaven like a turkey-cock on dress parade, forgotten aeons behind him, blank time before him, his birth a mystery, his death a leap in the dark; when I see him pose on the grave of forgotten races and puff himself up with pomposity like the frog in the fable; when I see him sprinkled with the dust of fallen dynasties and erecting new altars upon the site of forgotten fanes, yet staggering about under a load of dignity that would spring the knee joints of an archangel, I don't wonder that the Lord once decided to drown the whole layout like a litter of blind puppies.

Doctors

I have often wished that I was a doctor of medicine instead of a doctor of divinity. There's a strong affinity between the two professions. The D.D.s deal in faith and prayer, the M.D.s in faith and pills.

• • • • •

It's a curious coincidence that when the doctors began writing their prescriptions in Latin it quickly became a "dead language."

• • • • •

Let it be recorded to their eternal credit, that, whatever may be their faults, precious few of them will practice in their own families.

• • • • •

When doctors disagree the patient usually dies.

• • • • •

Methuselah lived 969 years—but that was before the development of the science of medicine.

• • • • •

I much doubt whether one-half the M.D.s now sending people to the drug stores with cipher dispatches, could tell what was the matter with a suffering mortal were he transparent as glass and lit up by electricity.

• • • • •

The medical profession is continually alarming the country. It has been but a little while since men were assured that they were poisoning their babies by kissing them. Havana cigars give a fellow the "tobacco heart," plug exhausts the saliva necessary to digestion, and bourbon whiskey burns his stomach full of blowholes. Beer makes him bilious, tea and coffee knock out his nerves, while plum pudding gives him dyspepsia, grape pie appendicitis, and hot biscuits undermine his general health. Emotional preaching afflicts him with "jerks," golf has a tendency to paresis, the round dance infects him with philogyny, and bicycling deforms his face. We might just as well be dead and with Lucifer as believe the doctors, for life wouldn't be half worth the living if we heeded their laws.

Dogmatism

Dogmatism is the fecund mother of doubt, a manacle on the human mind, a brake on the golden wheel of Christian progress; and every dogmatizer, whether in science, politics, or religion, is consciously or unconsciously, a Humbug. You know, do you? Know what? And who told you?

• • • • •

By presuming to know too much of God's great plan, by decrying intelligent criticism and attempting to seal the lips of living students with the dicta of dead scholastics, by standing ever ready to brand as blasphemers those who presume to question or dare to differ, the dogmatists are driving millions of God-fearing men into passive indifference or overt opposition.

• • • • •

There be people in this world who will not read a book or paper which does not reflect their preconceived ideas, or idiocies—lest they learn something. Their inordinate egotism, or rather their tergeminous gall, their three-ply impudence, leads them to assume that they have a corner on the wisdom of the world.

Doubt

The more a man knows the more he doubts.

• • • • •

It is not until a young man suspects he knows more than his father that he begins to doubt the religion of his mother.

• • • • •

Figure up how much you can prove that which you believe, and you'll find that you've got to go into intellectual bankruptcy.

O dammit!

Dudes

Feminine conceit, fed on flattery, were as milk shake unto mescal, as a kiss by mail to one by moonlight, compared with the insufferable egotism of the "pretty man" who puts his moustache up in curlpapers and perfumes his pompadour; who primps and postures before an amorous looking glass and imagines that all Eve's daughters are trying to abduct him. Whenever I meet one of these male irresistibles I'm forcibly reminded that the Almighty made man out of mud. . . .

E

Eden

Had man remained in Eden he would have been a chump forever.

Editors & Publishers

The "able editor" is perhaps the only quack doctor extant who greedily swallows his own medicine and foolishly imagines that it does him good. Puffery is the "able editor's" invariable prescription, no matter whether the patient be a moss-grown town, a broken down political roue, or a Cheap-John merchant suffering the first paroxysms of financial dissolution.

• • • • •

The feature of most interest to the lay reader is the political homilies of the editor himself. Not only are they deeply interesting to the hoi polloi, but invaluable from a therapeutical standpoint, being successfully employed in cases of itch, smallpox, etc., as a counter irritant. I opine that one of these read in a loud voice to an Egyptian mummy would result in its immediate resurrection.

• • • • •

The proofreader is the bane of genius. He recently made the *Santone Express* say "Kjizxjeayzjjspkti" when the editor doubtless means "Zjjspktiyzcjxzijk."

• • • • •

When a man fails at everything else he is apt to be seized with a yearning ambition to become an editor. He gets trusted for a shirttail full o' pied type, a pre-Raphaelite press, lays in a job lot of editorial "We's" and a sawdust cuspidor, girds up his loins, and begins to commence. He adorns himself with a long-tailed, hand-me-down Albert Edward and carries the Universe in his arms. He pokes his meddlesome proboscis into everything and gives oodles of advice, unasked. He may not have as much principle as a tomcat in rutting time, but he poses before all men as a "guardian of public morals." He imagines that an eager multitude sits up every night to catch the first dank copy of his little matutinal mistake—to see what he's got to say.

• • • • •

He has an idea that his miserable little Journalistic misfit is "making the town" and is entitled to great words of gratitude—that should his towline break the whole community would go awhooping to hades, the bottom would fall out of realty values, and the streets be overgrown with Johnson grass. So he toils and sweats and stinks—imagines that he is roosting on the top rung of the journalistic ladder when he hasn't even learned his trade. Finally, he falls through the bosom of his pantalettes. The sheriff levies on his stock of editorial "We's," the past sours, the office cat starves, spiders festoon the sawdust cuspidor, and the dust settles like a pall on his collection of worn type and wood-base railway cuts. The secondhand engine ceases to snort, the rat printers disperse, and the wheezy old cylinder press no longer alarms the neighborhood. But in a little while, another yap scrapes up $40 in cash, catches a sucker to endorse his note, and there's a renascence of the old plant.

Education

A little learning is a dangerous thing, but it is infinitely safer than none at all.

• • • • •

There is no more reason why the State should confer a profession upon a young man than that it should provide him with forty acres and a mule. Let it teach him to read; he then holds the key to all knowledge.

• • • • •

We pore over books too much and reflect too little; depend too much on others, too little upon ourselves. We make of our heads cold-storage warehouses for other people's ideas. Too many who fondly imagine themselves educated, much resemble Mark Twain's frog with its stomach full of shot—they are crushed to earth by the things they have swallowed.

England & The English

England is the modern Attila, the Scourge of God, the curse of the world. Her arrogance and insolence are only equaled by her conscienceless cupidity.

• • • • •

America has done more for the human race in a hundred and twenty years than has England in all her hoary centuries. We could buy the miserable little island, pay for it, and blow it at the moon, and the world would be none the worse.

• • • • •

The Royal beast of Britain has never forgotten that once upon a time an infant Republic held him up by the beard and beat the immortal ichor out of him.

• • • • •

Your "true born Englishman" is an ethnological *olla podrida* composed of the rag-tail and bob-tail of all God's universe.

• • • • •

Perhaps the most densely ignorant, the most hopelessly stupid people on earth are the English. The farming class of that country cannot so much as speak a civilized language. Each district has a barbarous gibberish peculiar to itself, and when people from the opposite shores of the 2x4 island meet, they have to make signs like different tribes of savages. The great bankers of England are Jews, its great merchants are Irish, its great manufacturers are Scotch, its reigning family is Dutch, while all its great authors and orators, soldiers and statesmen have been either Celts or of

Celtic extraction. The genuine "Anglo-Saxon" runs chiefly to beef and brutality and little to brains.

• • • • •

England has produced some really great men, but, like the hen that sat on the nest of doorknobs, it has taken her a terrible long time to bring off her brood.

• • • • •

Wine and women may be an American weakness; that of England seems to be brandy and boys.

Environment

It is chiefly a question of environment whether we grow up Catholics or Protestants, Republicans or Democrats, Populists or political nondescripts. And yet we adhere to opinions we have inherited with all the tenacity of a dog to a bone or an American miser to a ten-dollar bill.

Episcopalianism

Episcopalianism in America is like the presence of a pebble in the works of a watch.

Evolution

Neither angels nor asses are exempt from the law of evolution.

• • • • •

If we were generated by the laws of blind force, we have achieved the impossible—the creature has become greater than its creator!

• • • • •

The world is young; it must run its course. Our Heavenly Father did not create it as the Chinese make crackers—just to hear it pop. Not until its power to produce and nourish life is exhausted will the end be.

• • • • •

It is evidently not in accordance with the Divine Plan to make a perfect man for a starter, else God would have begun at the other end of the string—he would not have inaugurated the slow process of evolution, that shibboleth of the Atheist.

• • • • •

Science has shelved the Biblical theory of the Creation just as Copernicus shelved the Ptolemaic system of astronomy—simply that and nothing more. It has "interrogated" nature with some little success but has never grasped the Alpha and Omega, the beginning and the end. It finds forces in operation which it calls "natural laws," but cannot tell how these laws became operative. It cannot tell whence life came or whither it goes. And the Atheist, pondering these things, concludes that the universe is a dead machine—a *mecanique celeste*—which exhibits order without plan and exists without excuse.

F

Faith

As a man's faith is inherited, or formed for him by circumstances, he deserves little more credit or blame therefore than for the color of his hair or the size of his ears.

• • • • •

Faith is founded on fallible human judgment. A man believes thus and so, not necessarily because it is so, but because his head is built on a particular pattern or has had a peculiar class of phenomena filtered through it.

Family Budget

When times are hard a man's first stroke of economy is to cut down his monthly allowance to his lady and his Lord, his last a reduction in the quality of his liquor.

Fashion & Society

Were I so fortunate as to be the only man on earth—a love thorn 'mid half a billion blossoms—I should insist upon a renaissance of the Edenic fashion, when lovely woman was clothed only with a few fig leaves and freckles.

• • • • •

It is only women with pretty ankles who go shopping on windy days.

• • • • •

Every woman possessing a pretty ankle is heartily in favor of "dress reform."

• • • • •

The abbreviated skirt may be more healthful than the pyramidal petticoat, but it makes a woman an offensive freak, an eyesore to the artist, an uncanny nightmare to all men with a correct conception of the eternal fitness of things. The reckless display of personal charms by the woman of fashion—her double-entendre *decolleté*—is not calculated to promote elevation of thought or purity of action.

• • • • •

The Iconoclast is the official organ of Texas's uppertendom, the social monitor for the land of the toothsome maverick. It prescribes just how low ballroom corsages shall be cut, and how high bloomers may be worn. It's the court of last resort in all social controversies, the handbook of *Les grandes dames* and debutantes, the pink of propriety from whose ipse dixit le beau monde makes no appeal. To be mentioned in the society reports of *The Iconoclast* were equivalent to being presented at court, for it takes cognizance only of the *crème de la crème*—the skimmings of the social milk pan.

• • • • •

Fashionable mothers commit their children to the care of serving maids while they sail out to soirées and receptions—put their babes on a bottle while they swing 'round the social circle. No wonder their sons grow up sapheads, as destitute of backbone as a banana, as deficient in moral force as a firkin of fish. Think of an infant Napoleon nursing a rubber nozzle, of rearing a Brutus on patent baby food, of bringing a Hannibal up by hand! You can't do it.

• • • • •

Why, if I had a woman of that kind to wife—a fashionable butterfly whose heart was in her finery, . . . who neglected her home to train with a lot of intellectual tomtits whose glory was small talk; who saved her sweetest smiles for society and her ill temper for the family altar—I say, were I tied to that kind of female, do you know what I'd do? Eh? You don't? Well, neither do I.

O dammit!

• • • • •

Thousands are today sailing about in silk hats who are guiltless of undershirts, bedecked with diamonds while in debt to the butcher for the meat on their bones. Families that can scarcely afford calico flaunt Parisian finery, keep costly carriages, while there's a chronic hiatus in their cupboards—go hungry to bed six nights in the week that on the seventh they may spread a brave feast for fashionable fools. God help all such cattle! They are the natural breeders of criminals and courtesans, for in such an atmosphere children grow up mentally dwarfed and morally debased.

• • • • •

The woman who will sacrifice a songster on the altar of her vanity is wholly devoid of sentiment. There's no more music in her soul than in a ham sandwich, less poetry in her life than can be found in a horned frog. A bird on the bonnet means that the woman beneath it would embalm her baby and wear it as a brooch if Dame Fashion decreed it. A wise husband would hesitate to insure his life in favor of such a woman, for she'd pour hot lead in his ear or dope his dinner to secure the price of a new dress.

• • • • •

It is imperative that we have in our fashionable pulpits preachers who will harmonize with their *recherche* surroundings. Placing a hunchback, a cross-eyed man, or one with an amorphous snout like that of old Socrates amid the gorgeous trappings of a hundred thousand-dollar temple were an insufferable sin against the aestheticism of the age.

Football

I am not decrying football—I incline to the view that an occasional rough-and-tumble scrapping match in which there is imminent danger of black eyes, and even of broken bones, is good for a boy. I simply point out that as an intellectual game it not only ranks far below chess, billiards, and baseball, but does not even rise to a parity with pugilism.

• • • • •

Football requires neither the intellect nor the perfect organization which is *sine qua non* to success in our great "national game." Its chief requisites are long hair, leathery lungs, and abnormally developed legs. The game owes its popularity to the average boy's predilection for the brutal, his inherent animalism. Football has for ages been a favorite game with savages, while baseball is a product of civilization.

Foreordination

Foreordination is the foolish faith that before God created the universe and sent the planets whirling about the blazing sun; that before the first star gleamed in the black o'erhanging firmament or a single mountain peak rose from the watery waste, He calmly sat Him down and mapped out every act of mortal man—decreed every war and pestilence, the rise and fall of every nation, and fixed the date of every birth and death. That may be good "orthodoxy," but it is not good sense. I dare not accuse my Creator of being responsible for all the sin and sorrow, suffering and shame that since the dawn of history has bedewed the world with blood and tears.

France

France can be more kinds of a flamboyant damphool, more varieties of an unmitigated nuisance in a given time than any other nation that ever existed upon the earth. She is utterly incapable of preserving a middle course in anything, is either bumping her head against the stars or crawling through the slime of her own sewers. She is constant to one thing never—is the irresponsible weathercock of the universe. France is great, but it is the greatness of a madman.

Friendship

I am sometimes tempted to believe that the only friendship that will stand fire is that of a yellow dog for a pauper negro.

G

Galveston

Many a good man has gone wrong in Galveston. There's something about the dreamy beach, the softly murmuring waves, and the sensuous breeze that comes stealing across the brine burdened with the perfumes of the Spanish Main, calculated to make even a preacher loath to wait for the imperishable joys of the New Jerusalem. When to such poetic surrounds are added a hundred naiads, posing in abbreviated costume upon a shimmering strand that suggests the land of the Lotos-eaters, saving grace itself may fail or even a presiding elder slip his anchor and go floating—heaven knows where.

The Galveston News

I will wager the *Galveston News* $500—in gold—that it cannot demonstrate that it has printed, as editorial, one original idea during the past sixty days. (I haven't read the paper closely, but I know its editors.)

Genius

To genius more than aught else, perhaps, distance lends enchantment.

• • • • •

The genuine man of genius seldom begins to live until he's been dead some decades.

Georgia

Georgia has a Sunday law that may be called a howling jimhun. A man found working on the first day of the week can be fined a thousand dollars, driven in the chain gang a year, then imprisoned six months as a common felon. If he declines to work when ordered to do so by the contractor to whom his services are sold, he may be adjudged guilty of "insurrection" and comfortably hanged. No exception is made in the case of those who observe the seventh day of the week as the Sabbath, hence a Jew may be legally executed in Georgia who has nowise encroached upon the rights of others, but merely observed the law of his religion. Georgia ought to be expelled from the Union until it learns something of the genius of this government. A state with such a medieval monstrosity, such a statuary abnormality, ought to be annexed to the Kongo—or Kansas.

God

A belief in God, that the Universe is the result of design, is inherent in man.

• • • • •

If there be no reason in the Universe, how comes it that there is sentience in the ridiculous little mites that cling to the shell of one relatively insignificant planet—like microbes to a mammoth cheese?

• • • • •

Had God desired to personally manifest himself unto man, to deliver a code of laws, to establish a particular form of worship, it is reasonable to suppose that he would have done so in a manner that would have left no doubt in the mind of any man, of any age or clime, anent either his divinity or his desires.

• • • • •

What one man believes or disbelieves is a matter of little moment. If Deity exists, he would continue to exist did a universe deny him; if he exists not, then all the faith and prayers and sacrifices of a thousand centuries will not evolve him from the night of nothingness. There is or there is not a life beyond the grave, regardless of the denial of every atheist and the affirmation of every prophet.

• • • • •

Most religions profess a foundation of direct revelation by their Deity, and for proof thereof cite us to wondrous prodigies—the dead restored, mountains removed, storms allayed, and children begotten—quite unnecessarily, I think—without the assistance of an earthly father. In other words, we are asked to believe that God proved his prescience and power by reversing those very laws which he had framed for cosmic rule.

• • • • •

To some the God-idea is a necessity absolute. Without the belief in immortality, the dark shadow of impending doom would drive them mad. It is their sheet-anchor in storm and stress—the still small voice that cries peace to their troubled souls.

• • • • •

Only those of cold natures, of slow-pulsing blood, of weak affections, can stand by the graves of their dead and deny the Deity.

• • • • •

All that is, or was, or can be, is but the visible garment of God. I ask no written covenant with Him. I will trust God without requiring priests or prophets to endorse his note.

• • • • •

I have a theory—for which I am seeking no converts—that God elects to punish some here and others hereafter.

• • • • •

The strongest evidence we can adduce that the world is governed by a sentient being is the absolute necessity for his existence. Of what avail is the mighty Universe without him?

• • • • •

"Who made God?" Suppose, good sir, that I find thee an answer. Who will furnish thee with an intellect to understand it?

• • • • •

How will you comprehend the genesis of a God, when the wisest man for whom Christ died cannot tell why water runs down hill instead of up?

• • • • •

Nature with God is one miracle; nature without God is a multitude of miracles.

• • • • •

If there be no God, then is Creation a calamity; if there be a God and no immortality for man, then it is a crime.

• • • • •

What matters it whether we call our Creator Jehovah or Jupiter, Brahma or Buddha? Who knoweth the name by which the Seraphim address him?

• • • • •

If there be no Fatherhood of God, there can be no Brotherhood of Man.

God's Grace

By God's grace, I mean not the kind given as excuse for passing the contribution plate; not the so-called "gifts of the Holy Ghost" that make a woman want to swing her sunbonnet, holler with her mouth open, hug all the brethren, and chew the nether lip of the preacher, but a return to the Ark of the Covenant; a recognition of the fact that the soul is not the stomach.

• • • • •

By God's Grace, I mean not the kind you catch at camp meetings with sand-fleas, wood-ticks, and other gifts of the Holy Ghost; but rather an end everlasting to brummagem and make-believe, a recognition of the fact that the soul is not the stomach.

Government

I lay it down as an incontrovertible proposition that a people should never delegate political power which they may, without great inconvenience, exercise themselves.

• • • • •

The wonder is not that the American sovereign knows so little of the science of government but that he knows anything about it at all.

• • • • •

Representative government is the legitimate child of democracy; but if given free rein the impudent brat will never fail to dishonor its parent.

• • • • •

One great trouble with our government is that it is becoming too complex, too redundant. There is danger of its breaking down with its own weight. We must study to simplify it, to dispense with many of our present offices, instead of creating more. The number of our tax-eaters is becoming alarming. They already constitute a vast nonproduction army; their support is becoming a serious drain on American industry. We have too many laws and lawmakers; too much red tape that hinders rather than helps Justice in the manipulation of her sword and scales. Government, municipal, State, or National, is a corporation in which every citizen is a stockholder, sharing in the gains or losses.

• • • • •

We're governed entirely too much. About every fifth man you meet is a public servant of some sort, and you cannot get married or buried, purchase a drink or own a dog, except with a by-your-leave to the all-pervading law of the land. In some states suicide itself is an infraction of the criminal code, and if the police don't cut you down in time the preachers will send you to hell.

H

Heaven

Were this world perfect, what need of heaven?

• • • • •

As near as I can figure it out, the inhabitants of the New Jerusalem will consist of several million women—and just men enough to fill the municipal offices.

• • • • •

Our highest possible conception of Heaven is but the world we know made perfect. We cannot so much as think of it except by earthly symbols. It is an idealization of the real, an intensification of what we find best in this life most beautiful.

• • • • •

People who cannot find happiness here begin to look for it in heaven. Eternal beatitude is another ridiculous rainbow. Nirvana is nonsense.

• • • • •

How better can we describe Heaven than by calling it Content; Hell than by naming it Discontent? One man is contented with a crust—finds Heaven in half a loaf of black bread; another is discontent with a crown—finds Hell in the wardship of half a world.

• • • • •

Better, a thousand times better, the most cruel pain a "benevolent Deity" can inflict upon those who displease him, than enforced companionship with people who can be happy in Heaven while myriads suffer in Hell!

O dammit!

Hell

No doubt 60,000 Americans go to Hell every year, and quite deservedly, too, for that many Republicans die.

• • • • •

Having lived in Houston two years, I do not particularly object to heat.

• • • • •

I could not contemplate so many millions suffering endless torment without going to their assistance, although I knew myself powerless to abate one jot or tittle of their agony. I would want to carry them a few drops of water, to help trample out the flames, to shield the women and children from the rain of fire, to add my puny strength to that of men who for ages past have striven to beat down those iron doors!

• • • • •

Hell specialization is becoming a hobby with pulpit pounders. One has an idea—or he thinks he has—that the "rum demon" is hell's dynamics. Another goes daft on the subject of gambling and sees the prince of darkness in every euchre deck. Another gets a maggot in his miserable little cerebellum that horse racing or Sunday baseball is what is about to blow the cylinder head out of the heavenly locomotive and leave us tied up at the halfway house; still another that dancing is sending the world in hot haste to the devil; and so on through an interminable list of banalities, not one of which is prohibited by the Bible. If those notoriety-seeking sapheads would either go plant hogs or hang their hobbies on the hat rack the world at large would have more respect for religion. It is a pretty good plan for a preacher to stick to his text; but those raucous-throated pseudo-religious rooters do not adhere to the Bible, nor even to their creed, but go sloshing around in the vacua of their own vain imaginings like a bad smell in a hot skillet, or the quintessential extract of nothingness chasing itself through the eternal void. If Christ and the Apostles were on earth today, they would be flatly told by these biliouslivered bigots and super-sanctified Smart Alecs that many things they approved are a curse to mankind.

Heritage

Talent may be transmitted from father to son; but you can no more inherit genius than you can inherit a fall out of a balloon.

• • • • •

I always feel sorry for a man who's got nothing to be proud of but a dead gran'daddy, for it appears to be a law of nature that there shall be but one great man to a tribe—that the lightning of genius shall not twice strike the same family tree.

• • • • •

Men who were too proud to borrow leave sons who are not ashamed to beg.

Heretics

An heretic, my dear sir, is a fellow who disagrees with you regarding something with which neither of you know anything about.

Heroes

One catfish does not make a creek, nor one hero a nation. The waves do not make the sea, but the sea furnishes forth the waves.

• • • • •

Victory does not always proclaim the hero nor virtue the saint.

• • • • •

Let the heroes of history have their due; still I imagine the world will have been much the same had Alexander died of cholera infantum or grown up a harmless dude.

O dammit!

• • • • •

Any man may be a hero when surrounded by the pomp and circumstance of war—when the cheers of contending thousands, the roar of batteries, and the crash of steel breeds murder in the blood.

• • • • •

The man who can grow in grace while his pet corn's in chancery, or lose an election without spraining his moral character; who can sit an hour for his dinner without walking all over the nerves of his wife, or crawl out of a bed in the middle of his first nap and rustle till the cold, gray dawn with a brace of colicky kids, without broadly insinuating that he was a copper-riveted, nickel-plated, automatic, double-cylinder idiot ever to get married, is a greater hero than he that taketh a city.

• • • • •

The hero is not he that strives with the world for witness, who seeks the bubble fame at the cannon's brazen throat, and risks his life that he may live forever. To find out heaven in others' happiness and for their sake to sacrifice, and suffer wrongs that might be righted with a thread of steel; to live an honest life in a land where Truth doth feed on crusts, while Falsehood fattens at Lucullan feasts, requires more moral stamina, more true manliness, than to follow a flag into the very jaws of Hell, or die for the faith in the *auto-da-fé*.

Honesty

I've learned that you can't judge a man by his catechism.

• • • • •

The smart rascal is ever honest within the law—infamous in strict accord with the criminal code. The man once declared a bankrupt may become a multimillionaire, see people he settled with at 15 cents on the dollar die in the poorhouse, decline to pay them their just dues, and still be legally honest; but if you lend him a chew o' tobacco you had best take a receipt for it.

• • • • •

I have noticed that shouting hosannahs has no tendency to make one more truthful in a horse trade.

• • • • •

There are many church people who will slander you unmercifully for dissenting from their religious dogma, then seize the first opportunity to stick you with a plugged dime or steal your dog.

The Houston Post

The stench of such a paper creeps abroad like the malodor of a cloaca, beslimes the senses like the noxious exhalations of an open sewer.

• • • • •

How in God's name men can be found so debased as to work on such a sheet is beyond my comprehension. I once undertook to hold down its editorial page; but soon "got sore at myself," cursed everything connected therewith, from the pink-haired president of the company to the business manager, got out, purified myself, and have been sick at the stomach ever since.

• • • • •

All that I now see of the paper is the clippings sent me by disgusted Houstonians, and I take those out behind the barn to read—then bury them lest they poison the hogs.

• • • • •

The "personal columns" of the *Post* was, by all odds, the foulest, filthiest, and most damnably disgusting thing to be found in American journalism. In it old libertines advertised for school-girl victims and pickled prostitutes made brazen bids for business.

• • • • •

It does seem that the *Post* will do anything for a dollar—except be decent. It is a social leper, a journalistic pariah. It is devoid of political principle as a thieving tomcat of conscience. It is a perfect maelstrom of misinformation, the avatar of impudence, the incarnation of infamy—a social cesspool whose malodor spreads contagion like the rank breath of the Gila monster or the shade of a upas tree. Yet its editor, I am told, aspires to the lieutenant-governorship of Texas. Verily, he's "got his gall."

The Human Race

Do the people of this Western World find life sweeter, better with the living in the last quarter of the nineteenth century than they did in the first quarter of the eighteenth? No! In God's great name, no! Our boasted progress is but a mighty agitation of that great ocean of humanity which sends the lighter particles to the top as froth and foam, there to catch the prismatic colors of the sun, while the great mass surges sullen beneath, the only hope of each particular particle that it too may become foam and float to the sunny surface of that dark, troubled sea.

• • • • •

I do not believe that we can pick ourselves up by our embroidered bootstraps and hop blithely astride a millennium built to order; but I do believe that the human race is slowly but surely working the subsoil out of its system, is becoming ever less the beast and more the god.

• • • • •

A thousand years are to the Lord as but one day, and by laborious inquiry and shrewd guesswork, we can trace the Human Race back almost a week.

• • • • •

The existence of the Human Race is but an unimportant incident in the history of the Universe. "Lords of Creation"—Forsooth! We are idle sport of time and space.

Humbugs

The American People, as P. T. Barnum long ago pointed out, have a weakness for humbugs. They are the natural prey of the charlatan, and in nothing more so than in matters Political. Despite their boasted intelligence, they will follow with a trust that partakes of the pathetic the mountebank who can perform the most slight-of-hand tricks, the demagogue who can make the most noise.

• • • • •

We are humbugs because we desire that our fellows think us better, braver, brighter, perhaps richer, than we really are.

I

•••••••••••••••••

Ideas

When you get an idea, don't run off into the woods with it lest somebody take it away from you. Put it on the anvil and bid the world hit it with the heaviest sledge.

•••••

You no more can get a large idea into a small head than you can put Pike's Peak into a pint cup.

Ignorance

The less a man knows the more he despises knowledge.

•••••

Ignorance is but intellectual infancy.

•••••

Optimism is a delightful thing, but is too frequently the result of ignorance.

•••••

Ignorance is not a crime per se, but it is the mother of Superstition and Intolerance, those twin demons that have time and again deluged the world with blood and tears, that for forty centuries have stood like ravenous wolves in the path of human progress.

Immortality

The fact that man desires immortality is proof enough that he was not born to perish.

Robert Ingersoll, Atheist

He says nothing, but does it so entertainingly that we long to hear him say it again.

• • • • •

Read three of Ingersoll's lectures and you get all he ever said—and every bit of it was borrowed.

• • • • •

Ingersoll is as guiltless of original ideas as a rabbit, but is an expert at putting old wine into new bottles.

• • • • •

An ignoramus believes the Bible because of the miracles, and because of the miracles an Ingersoll disbelieves it—and both are equally blind.

Insults

Miss Bloodgood was resplendent in a rich gown of lilac silk, the corsage cut *à la chemise,* and displaying carefully barbered arms possessing all the grace and charm so much admired in the living skeleton.

• • • • •

In bowing her acknowledgments, Miss Bloodgood had the misfortune to spill herself out of her corsage, upon which a fair debutante from Temple, with the naïveté of a little child, observed *sotto voce,* that "a bust of that kind should be carried in a bucket."

• • • • •

Had Queen Elizabeth worn bloomers, Sir Walter Raleigh might have bridged a mud puddle for her with his costly cloak; but more likely he would have told her to climb upon his back.

• • • • •

She has three lovely children, one of whom is thought to resemble her husband.

O dammit!

• • • • •

He declares that an Irishman is a man born in Ireland, a Scotchman a man born in Scotland, but does not insist that a kitten born in an oven becomes a loaf of bread.

• • • • •

He now turns the other cheek to the smacker and gets it smuck.

• • • • •

He looms up like a two-dollar skyrocket on a dark night.

• • • • •

[New York Socialite Ruth Hanna] is only in her seventeenth year, but . . . is quite big for her size.

• • • • •

Doubtless God made him [J. B. Cranfill, Editor, *Baptist Standard*]; it follows, therefore, that he should pass for a man. The Architect of the Universe may have had some remnants left over—*disjecta membra* of various mammalia. Nature wastes nothing; hence, what more likely than that the Creator should throw these remnants together and call it Cranfill.

• • • • •

[M. D. Early, Baptist Minister] insisted that he had never read a copy of *The Iconoclast* and would not do so, yet declared it awfully immoral, which proves that Early is a great man. He does not have to acquire knowledge by a patient industry like other people, but takes it by absorption as the sponge does stale beer on a mahogany bar, and when he wants to leak it he has only to squeeze his nice soft head.

• • • • •

Johann Jakob [John Jacob Astor] came to America in the steerage, wearing a Limburger linsey-woolsey and a pair of wooden shoes. Beginning life in the new world as a rat-catcher, he soon acquired a gallon jug of Holland gin, a peck of Brummagem jewelry, and robbed the aborigines right and left. He wore the same shirt year 'round, slept with his dogs, and invested his *groschens* in such Manhattan dirt as he could conveniently transport upon his person.

• • • • •

John Churchill, founder of the House of Marlborough, was the Boss Tweed of his time, the prize pimp of his day and generation. As a traitor he was the peer of Judas Iscariot, and he has been equaled in shameless dishonesty by his lineal descendants. The only assurance we have that the latter were not bastards is to be found in the fact that they were one and all stamped from head to heel with the Marlborough meanness.

• • • • •

Anna [Gould] found the "count" on the matrimonial bargain counter and gathered him in—paid for him, much as one might purchase a hairless Mexican pup.

• • • • •

Mrs. Bradley-Martin does not exactly "look every inch a queen," her horizontal having developed at the expense of her perpendicular, suggesting the rather robust physique of her father's beer barrels. Still, she is not an attractive woman, having the ruddy complexion of an unlicked postage stamp.

• • • • •

The Sunday World boasts a tremendous circulation, and I can easily believe it—when I consider the large population of our lunatic asylums. [It] can spoil more white paper with jejune babble and abortive art than any other publication on earth—with the possible exception of the *Houston Post*. It is slop from imprimis to finis, but slop made from pouring port and keg beer, absinthe and barrelhouse booze into the same bowl.

• • • • •

[The Reverend T. DeWitt] Talmage is troubled with a diarrhea of words and should take something for it. He is simply a monstrous bag of fetid wind. The man who can find intellectual food in Talmage's sermons could acquire a case of delirium tremens by drinking the froth out of a pop bottle.

Mr. Talmage should retire to some secluded spot and make a careful analysis of his sermons before firing them at the press. They may sound all right in the big tabernacle, where a great volume of noise is the chief desideratum, but they make very poor reading. Like a flapjack, they may tickle the palate when served hot and with plenty of "sop"; but when allowed to grow cold are stale, flat, and unprofitable.

• • • • •

My attention has just been called to a little New York paper called *Life*. How the poor thing ever managed to get so far from home I cannot imagine, unless some crockery jobber used it in packing a consignment of Yellow thundermugs which he was sending to Texas. I thought I had seen all New York's journalistic freaks, from the *Police Gazette* down to *Town Topics*, but *Life* is one abnormality which I had hitherto overlooked. I shall place this copy in my cabinet of curios, it being the only journal on earth having absolutely no shadow of excuse for existing. It is too stupid to be witty, too ignorant to impart information, too epicene to be even immoral. It suggests a castrated donkey that is too spiritless to bray, too lazy to die, and simply leans against a post and slobbers.

• • • • •

Town Topics is what is known in the terse vernacular of Hungry Hill and Tincan Alley as a journalistic "nancy"—a trifle too dirty for decency and too epicene for aggressive immortality. It is one of those papers which an imbecile may understand much better than a man of strong mentality, because the latter seeks a *raison d'être* for everything. Its distinguished feature is a dreary waste of inane tittle-tattle anent the doings and misdoings of uppertendom. It can tell you to the minute when the charming, beautiful, and accomplished Miss Isolde De Peyster Hamfat-Crupper became engaged to the redoubtable Count Orlando Bombastic Furioso Marraroni de Cagliostro, how many buttons she will wear on the bifurcated garment of her wedding lingerie, and whether the broken windows in the count's ancestral castle are stuffed with old hats or baled hay. It knows how often J. J.Van Allen changes his sox and with what material the exuberant basement of T. Suffern Tailor's riding breeches are half-soled—information in nowise to be despised in this era boasting itself heir of all the ages. It should be the official organ of every suicide club in the country, being well calculated to disgust every sane man with the whole human race and make him desire a speedy death.

• • • • •

[Populist Party leaders] . . . Cryptogram Donnelly, Keep-Off-the-Grass Coxey, Caught-in-a-Lie Bateman . . . over whom any dog might be well proud to lift a leg.

• • • • •

[Evangelist Sam Small] has no more conception of what the Bible really is than a hog has of Hebrew. If sure enough men were selling for a million dollars each in the open market, Sam Small would not bring a dime done up in packages of a dozen.

• • • • •

[Evangelist Sam Jones] O Jonesy, Jonesy! Would to heaven that thou and all thy brother blabsters and bubbly-jocks would go hang yourselves, for you know naught of the war that rages ever like a sulphurous siroc in the human soul. Ye are but insects that infest great Igdrasyl, the ash tree that upholds the universe.

• • • • •

Yes, I've read it [*Quo Vadis*], and when I had finished the miserable thing my head felt as though full of wind and dishwater. *Quo Vadis* is the mental mooncalf, a chaotic *olla podrida* composed of the intellectual fag ends of the universe. It is a conglomeration of meaningless words, a concatenation of absurdities, a cataclysm of nascence and nonsense. Reading it were like seining the Atlantic to find a bullfrog.

• • • • •

Chauncey Depew has again permitted his mouth to go off prematurely. This time he told ambitious young Americans how to get on Easy Street. It's dead easy—all you have to do is double the usefulness of electricity, discover a wonderful gold mine, or invent a successful flying machine! If you remain poor with this open-sesame to opulence concealed about your person you deserve no pity. Chauncey reminds me more and more of Artemus Ward's monkey—he's such an "Amoosin Kuss"; and he's never so excruciatingly funny as when he takes himself seriously. Besides being America's most distinguished pantophagist, post-prandialist, and paneulogist, Dr. Depew is a pantascopic pansophical pantaloon. Like a Persian dervish, he can, by gazing steadfastly into his own umbilicus, see wondrous visions of things yet to be. He says that we are going to have better times—by and by. I had suspected something of the sort myself.

• • • • •

As an editor he is a dismal failure, but he would be a dazzling success as ballast for a canal boat.

• • • • •

Ye gods! Has American journalism come to this? *O tempora! O mores!* O mama! The great heart of *The Iconoclast* bleeds for Houston's unfortunate [newspaper] . . . now brought so low that the very dogs no longer pause in front of her office, despite the seductive sign, *Houston Post.*

• • • • •

Of course it were easy to suggest that the mother of this mental abnormality [Dr. Geo. D. Taylor of Los Angeles] expends much time scratching fleas with her hind feet, but the dog is man's best friend, and to accredit Taylor with so decent an origin were fulsome flattery.

• • • • •

I can but wonder what will become of the [*Los Angeles*] *Times* editor when the breath leaves his feculent body and death stops the rattling of his abortive brain, for he is unfit for heaven and too foul for hell. He cannot be buried in the earth lest he provoke a pestilence, nor in the sea lest he poison the fish, nor swung in space like Mahomet's coffin lest the circling worlds in trying to avoid contamination, crash together, wreck the universe, and bring again the noisome reign of Chaos and old Night. The damn rascal seems to be a white elephant on the hands of Deity, and I have some curiosity to know what He will do with it.

• • • • •

The portrait—which I sincerely hope does Miss Garesche rank injustice—makes her dish-faced as a new moon, with nose like a seed wart, weak mouth, soup-ladle chin, and a smirk calculated to frighten anything but a French count sorely in need of cash.

• • • • •

Mrs. Crupper's beauty is that voluptuous type known to the Euphuists as Junoesque but called by the vulgar herd Oleomargaramic.

• • • • •

[Texas Governor Charles Culberson] Chollie Boy has the abnormal taste for public pap, but a lesser brain and as little political conscience as a raccoon. He's so selfish and cold-blooded that he's actually clammy. He would rattle in a senatorial toga like a navy bean in a bushel basket, be as hopelessly lost as a tabby cat clad in the skin of an Asiatic elephant. Senator Cholly Boy Culberson! Ye Gods and Little Fishes! *O tempora! O mores!* O hell!

• • • • •

When [society snobs] get to Heaven they will refuse to associate with Jesus Christ because he was a carpenter, and turn up their patrician proboscides at Almighty God for having worked in mud.

J

Judaism

A Christian world does not remember that the Jews gave birth to Christ, but never forgets that they crucified him.

• • • • •

To deny that there is a widespread antipathy to the Jew were as fatuous as to deny the existence of the sun. In "Christian" Russia the Jews are being despoiled and outraged—their homes given to the flames, their savings to the plunderer, their daughters to the ravisher, their throats to the knife! And the rest of the so-called Christian world mildly protests, intimates that, perhaps, after all, the Jew has a soul, at least flesh and bone, and may suffer somewhat.

• • • • •

For twenty centuries the Jew has been the target at which the finger of scorn was ever pointed; the buffet of dissolute princes and purse-proud potentates; the undeserving victim of the blind wrath of the proletarian rabble; the mark at which sectarian hate and unreasoning bigotry have leveled their most vindictive shafts; despoiled, outraged, beaten, expatriated, driven hither and thither, finding no rest for his weary feet in a world which his wisdom has done so much to humanize, to which he has given the happiness here and hope hereafter.

• • • • •

When our ancestors were but brutal barbarians, clad in skins stripped with sharp stones from beasts scarcely less ferocious; dwelling in caves and subsisting on roots and raw meat; with no aspirations above the crudest creature comforts, no conception of immortality, no dream of man's high destiny, the Jews were worshipping the "Lord of Hosts," framing those laws which are today the basic principle of civilization, weaving into the woof of human history those imperishable gems of poesy and philosophy which the world's wisest say transcend the genius of mortal man and must, perforce, be the gracious gift of God.

Journalism

"New Journalism"—Rats! Ditto rodents!

• • • • •

Journalism is no esoteric science; it is as "easy as lying."

• • • • •

Really, it were as fatuous to establish schools of Journalism as to found professorships for instruction in the art of making chile-con-carne or bad smells.

K

Kansas

There everything goes by contraries. The cows lay eggs and the hens give milk. Apples are dug out of the earth and potatoes grow on trees. Dogs wear feathers and geese grow hair. The sun rises in the west and sets at noon, while the Fourth of July comes in the middle of January.

• • • • •

The Kansas people are the incarnation of industry. This is because the average citizen of that commonwealth expends all his nervo-muscular resources attending to everybody's business but his own. Kansas is the country of the crank, the abiding place of the professional reformer. The Kansan is full of the idea that he is his brother's keeper. You can't shove a wire through any keyhole in Kansas without putting out the eye of a he-angel. The Kansan is born with a religious belly-ache of which he never gets rid until the goes down to the grave. He is preeminently powerful in prayer and his amen fairly drips with unction; but you can't trust him in a horse trade. He imagines that those who are not so meddlesome and miserable as himself are foredoomed to hell.

• • • • •

There are said to be some people in Kansas so cold-blooded that their children are born with frost on 'em, and whose only recreation is chewing gum.

Kansas City

I chanced some time ago to spend a couple o'days in Kansas City, a bustling little place situated at the mouth of the Kaw, and somewhat celebrated as headquarters for the jug trade of Kansas. It is also distinguished for the size of its pork packeries. The [coat of] arms of Kansas City are a gallon jug rampant, a fat porker regardant, a blood pudding couchant, and the motto, "There's nothing like licker and lard." I am told that its swagger set still attend its social functions sans coats and collars, feed themselves with knives and for napkins use the corners of the tablecloth. Kansas City is a big, blustering, uncouth, and uncultured "yap" town. The elite of Kansas City run very little to art and literature. Their pantheon is a pork packery and Phil D. Armour their Olympian Jove. Their hero is the man who can stick the most pigs in a given number of minutes, and their popular melodies are a variation of the death squeal of that homely but useful animal. The Jesse James dime novel and the New York "yaller" newspapers suffice to satisfy Kansas City's rather moderate longing for literature. As might be expected, the press of Kansas City is a true reflex of its life—stupid, ignorant, and obstinate as the hog upon which the commercial greatness of the place is grounded.

L

Law

We have one law for the retail and another for the wholesale robber.

• • • • •

During the year 1894 there were about 9,800 homicides and but 132 legal executions reported in the United States. As matters now stand, one might slay a fellow mortal every year and stand an excellent chance of dying of old age, so far as the courts are concerned. You may go upon the streets, insult a man, provoke him to offer you violence, shoot him down like a dog, and, if able to employ eminent counsel to behedge you with legal technicalities and befuddle the jury, go scot free; or failing in that, put the public to an expense of several thousand dollars in excess of what your cowardly carcass is worth, and escape with a short term in some comfortable penitentiary, where you will be well cared for, taught a good trade, and regularly prayed for at the expense of law-abiding people.

• • • • •

We select as jurors, not those who know most about the case, but those who know least. When an atrocious crime is committed we set aside as unavailable those who have kept in touch with current events, and select a jury from the residue. As a rule, we get together twelve of the most consummate blockheads in the country, permit them to be further obfuscated by artful counsel, then lock them up until the most obstinate jackass in the corral dominates the herd or compels a compromise.

• • • • •

The man hanged for homicide usually repents and is jerked to Jesus, while his victim, cut off in the heyday of his sins, is supposed to go to hell a-whopping.

I would wipe out our entire penal code and frame a new one in which there would be no comfortable penitentiaries. If a man were found guilty of rape or homicide I'd promptly hang him, if of a less heinous offense I'd give him stripes proportionate to his crime and turn him loose to earn a livelihood and thus prevent his family becoming a public burden.

Lawyers

There are good lawyers and good preachers—but they are not numerous.

• • • • •

Our courts have become mere circumlocution offices, winding and unwinding red tape, instead of the sinewy arm of justice wielding the unerring sword. Our judges are usually learned and upright, our juries eager to administer justice, our officers active and the public heart in the right place; but it avails not—our system is all wrong. We make too many laws, then involve them in a mass of legal verbiage which permits a skilled sophist to demonstrate to the untrained mind that they mean what best serves the interest of his client. It is common cant that "the people make the laws." They do not. The lawyers make them, and that with the full understanding that the more intricate the legal machinery may be, the more need of experts, the fatter the harvest of fees. All the criminal laws this country needs could be printed in a pamphlet no larger than *The Iconoclast,* together with full instructions for their enforcement.

• • • • •

The little tinhorn attorney, whose specialities are divorce and libel suits, who is ever for sale to the highest bidder—keeps tears on tap for whosoever will drop a dollar in the slot; will weep over the woes of the red-handed homicide or bewail the gaping wounds of his victim; will take a contingent fee to bleed his best friend, or enter into a conspiracy to despoil honest industry by due process of law; will rob the orphan of his patrimony on a legal technicality and brand the Virgin Mary as a bawd to shield a blackmailer—well, he can't be put in the penitentiary, more's the pity! But it's some satisfaction to believe that if, in all the great universe of God there is a Hell where fiends lie howling, the most sulfurous section is reserved for the infamous shyster, the carrion crow of human kind—that if he cannot be debarred from the courts of earth he'll get the bounce from those of Heaven.

• • • • •

It is not absolutely necessary that a lawyer should be a rascal.

Lies & Liars

A really artistic liar is not exactly the noblest work of God, but next to an honest politician, he is, perhaps, the rarest.

• • • • •

The Lord once attempted to check the lying habit by striking falsifiers dead, but soon saw that such a plan would prove more destructive than another deluge—that there wouldn't be even a Noah's ark picnic party of us left.

• • • • •

I do not feel altogether qualified to write a manual on the art of lying—albeit I was for some years editor of the *San Antonio Express.*

• • • • •

Oh, people are becoming such incorrigible liars that I've about quit trying to borrow money.

Life

Of suffering and sorrow were born all life's beauty. Nations rise through a mist of tears. Every great lifework is an agony. Behind every song there lurks a sigh. There's an element of sadness in humor itself. The Virgin Mother is known as Our Lady of Pain. The first beat of life and the last gasp are drawn in suffering, and between the cradle and the grave there lies a monster-haunted Sahara.

• • • • •

Life has a limited circulation and no assurance of a second edition.

• • • • •

With the most of us life at its best is no luxury, but a fierce struggle from the cradle to the grave—days of toil and anxiety, suffering and sin, with here and there a bright oasis redolent with the song of birds and the perfume of a thousand flowers.

• • • • •

Life seems no longer real, no longer earnest, but a made farce, a Momus masque, wherein Genius panders to the gross appetites of gilded fools and the world is ruled by the impudence of wealth. All the melody of life is drowned by the wrangling of the money changers, and the social hullabaloo of fashionable harlots; the roses are trampled ruthlessly into the mire in the mad race for riches, virtue has become a byword and honor a reproach.

• • • • •

Unfortunately, the lunatic is in love with life.

Love

Love is really a very serious thing. Like seasickness, everybody laughs at it but the fellow that's got it.

• • • • •

It is—O dammit! It's that which transforms a snub-nosed dairy maid into a Grecian goddess, a bench-legged farmer boy into a living Apollo.

• • • • •

Love is the most sacred word ever framed by celestial lips. It's the law of life, the harmony of heaven, the breath of which the universe was born, the divine essence increate of the ever-living God. But love is like all other sweet things—unless you get the very best brand it sours awful easy.

• • • • •

There is none immune, and the best of us will sometime nibble at love's hook when baited with a sunbonnet and a pair of bloomers.

• • • • •

To the best of my knowledge and belief, love will pick a man up quicker and throw him down harder than even the double-distilled brand of Prohibition busthead.

• • • • •

When I love a woman I love her up one side and down t'other. I may be an uncultured and barbaric noodle, but I want to get hold of her and bite her neck. I want to cuddle her sunny curls on my heaving shirtfront when I talk to her about affinities. I believe with Tennyson in the spirits rushing together at the touching of the lips, and I just let them rush.

M

Man

Many a man swears because he's too proud to weep, hides a quivering soul behind a cynic's sneer, fronts the world like a savage beast at bay while his heart's a fathomless lake of tears.

• • • • •

The place to take the true measure of a man is not the forum or the field, not the marketplace or the amen-corner, but at his own fireside. There he lays aside his mask and you may judge whether he's imp or angel, king or cur, hero or humbug. I care not what the world says of him—whether it crown him with bays or pelt him with bad eggs; I care never a copper what his reputation or religion may be. If his babes dread his homecoming and his better-half swallows her heart every time she has to ask him for a five-dollar bill, he's a fraud of the first water, even though he prays night and morn till he's black in the face, and howls hallelujah till he shakes the eternal hills.

• • • • •

Man is nothing if not contrary.

• • • • •

Man has a tendency to become what he believes himself to be. Consciously or unconsciously, he strives with less or greater strength toward his ideal; hence it is all-important that he consider himself an immortal rather than the pitiful sport of Time and Space. Had man always considered himself simply an animal, his tendencies would have been ever earthward; believing himself half divine, he has striven to mount above the stars.

O dammit!

• • • • •

Man is just like a dog—only more so.

• • • • •

Men are but children who have had the mumps.

Mankind

We are but accidents, spawn of the sun and slime, each an Ishmael considering only himself.

• • • • •

Many of our so-called great men are but featherless geese, possessing a superabundance of gall—creatures of chance, who ride, like pieces of driftwood, on the crest of a wave, raised by forces they cannot comprehend; but they ride and the world applauds them, while it tramples better men beneath its brutal feet.

• • • • •

Surely, the stupendous labors of the Creator were undertaken with grander object, a nobler aim than the breeding on this comparatively unimportant planet of a few harpers for Heaven and a host of hoodlums for Hell.

• • • • •

Millions make continual moan that they are not happy when they ought to be thankful that they are not hanged. I'd make good Baptists of the whole caboodle—would hold them under water long enough to soak out the original sin. A man complains because Fortune doesn't empty her cornucopia into the pockets of his pantalettes while he whittles a pine box and talks municipal politics instead of humping himself behind an enterprising mule in the cotton patch. If his sweetheart jilts him, he's in despair, and if she marries him he wishes he were dead. It seems never to have occurred to these Westerian wailers that the happiest existence is that of the lower animals—that the human being of fine brain and keen sensibilities cannot possibly be content. It is this very unrest, this heart-hunger that drives a man on to noble deeds—that lifts him out of the gutter where wallow the dull, dumb beasts and places him among the gods. Of suffering and sorrow were born all life's beauty.

• • • • •

We imagine that because we no longer live in caves and fight naked with the wild beasts of the forest for our food we are away up at the head of the procession.

• • • • •

If the acorn falls upon the rock it perishes; if upon the fruitful soil it becomes a spreading oak. Whether it lives or dies matters but little, for acorns are many and the genus runs ever on. So with the life of man.

• • • • •

How small we are, how ephemeral, how helpless in God's great hand! Is it not strange that we do not cling, each to the others, like shipwrecked mariners riding the stormy waters on some frail raft and looking with dilating eyes into the black abyss?—that we waste our little lives in wild wars and civic strife?—that all our souls are concentrated in that one world, selfishness?—that we have time to hate?

Man As Polygamist

It is well to ever bear in mind that man is by nature a Mormon.

Man & Woman

Whatever may have been Eve's fortune, Adam was no great loser by being ejected from Eden, for the man who possesses the love of a good woman carries Paradise with him wherever he goes.

• • • • •

A woman talks to entertain her companions; man gabs for no other evident reason than to air his ignorance.

• • • • •

Paradoxical as it may appear, woman is at once the subject and the sovereign of man, his inferior and superior, mentally and physically.

• • • • •

"Can woman hypnotize man?" Well, I should snigger. She can hypnotize anything that wears pants, from the prince at his gilded poker game, to the peasant scattering worm poison in the lowly cotton patch and revolving in his think tank the tenets of Populism. She hypnotizes because she can't help it. She's built that way.

Marriage

The institution of marriage, like the law against theft, was originally intended to guarantee to each male member of the community peaceable possession and enjoyment of his property.

• • • • •

Marriage is, perhaps, the only game of chance ever invented at which it is possible for both players to lose.

• • • • •

Pope calls man the "great lord of all things"—but Pope never got married.

• • • • •

What man hath joined man may put asunder.

• • • • •

Marriage is nothing more or less than formal notification to the world that a man and woman have already become husband and wife. It matters not how this announcement is made, so long as due respect is shown the established customs of the world. There's naught more sacrosanct in the act of Church or state in so far as the marriage ceremony is concerned than in the newspaper notice of its consummation.

• • • • •

My observation has been that most matches are made in about this manner: By some horrible accident John Hennery and Sarah Jane become acquainted. They have no more "affinity" than a practical politician and pure spring water; but they dance and flirt, fool around the front gate in the dark of the moon, sigh and talk nonsense. John Hennery begins to take things for his breath and Sarah Jane for her complexion. The young goslings get wonted to each other, and the first thing you know they're tied up till death or divorce doth them part. And had Sarah Jane missed John Hennery altogether she would have been just as well—perhaps better—content with some other fellow, while he would have found a different mother-in-law and made as enthusiastic a failure of married life.

• • • • •

One expects to capture a demigod who hits the earth only in high places; the other to wed a wingless angel who will make his Edenic bower one long-drawn sigh of ecstatic bliss. The result is that one is tied up to a slattern who slouches around the house with her hair on tins, in a dirty collar and with a dime novel, a voice like a catfight; the other a hoodlum who comes home from the lodge at 2 A.M. and whoops and howls for her to come down and hunt for the keyhole, and is then snailed in by a policeman before she can frame a curtain lecture or find the rolling pin.

Medicine

Faith is the basic principle of both medicine and miracles.

Methodists

The Methodist Episcopal Conference, recently assembled in New York, created something of a sensation by rejecting a candidate for clerical honors because he was cross-eyed. Many worthy brethren have sharply criticized the action of the conference, but *The Iconoclast* is inclined to commend it. No man who can look two ways at once has any business in the Methodist ministry.

Miscellaneous

The average human head, like an egg, or a crock of clabber, absorbs the flavor of its surroundings.

• • • • •

The luxuries of one generation become the necessities of the next.

• • • • •

Had Alexander been called "Willie" he could never have conquered the world.

• • • • •

The foolishest man alive knows that a Stradivarius cannot be whittled out of a cornstalk.

• • • • •

If those who dance must pay the piper, those who laugh must pay the jester.

• • • • •

Only the useful are successful.

• • • • •

Those who build are competent to destroy.

• • • • •

It is difficult for a man to get too much of a really good thing.

• • • • •

That man who has never known shoes needs none.

• • • • •

When godalmighty shapes a man's head like a bedpan we can hardly expect it to hold much that is valuable.

• • • • •

Next in value to knowing how to do a thing is knowing how not to do it.

• • • • •

An insanity expert thinks everybody crazy but himself.

• • • • •

Men demand the real, the tangible; infants, physical and mental, are satisfied with shadows.

• • • • •

How can you spoil a rotten egg? . . .

• • • • •

Gunpowder is a great promoter of good manners.

Missionaryism

That religion which sits up nights to agonize because a few naked [natives] in equatorial Africa never heard Eve's snake story, how Job scratched himself with a broken pie-plate, or the hog happened to be so full o' the spirit of Hades; that robs childhood of its pennies to send prayer books to people whose redemption should begin with a bath, while in our country every town from Cape Cod to Kalamazoo, every city between the Arctic Ocean and the Austral sea is filled with "Heathen" who know naught of the grace of God or the mystery of a square meal, is an arrant humbug—a crime against man, an offense to God, a curse to the world.

• • • • •

We sent to the famine-sufferers many Bibles and hymn-books, little bacon and beans. Bibles and hymnbooks are excellent things in their ways, but do not possess an absorbing interest for a man with an aching voice concealed in his system. Starving people ask a Christian world for grub, and it gives them forty 'leven different brands of saving grace, most of these elixirs of life ladled out by hired missionaries who serve God for the long green, and who are often so deplorably ignorant that they couldn't tell a religious thesis from an ichthyosaurian.

O dammit!

• • • • •

China will be compelled to accept the Bible at the muzzle of a blunderbuss—the Christian world will hold her and cram it down her throat with a bayonet.

• • • • •

The religion of the Turks and Chinese is just as dear to them as that of the Christian cult to its communicants; yet missionaries from Europe and America go among them uninvited and tell them that the time-honored faith of their fathers is but a tissue of falsehoods, their sacred rites but heathenish customs born of brutish ignorance, their prophets brazen impostors, their priests mere pretenders, and themselves the blind servants of Perdition's powers.

• • • • •

I defy any man to prove that one person is really converted from idolatry to Christianity for each million dollars collected in this country in the name of foreign missions.

• • • • •

It will be time enough to carry Bibles to barbarians when our own children are provided with bread.

• • • • •

In our own America the Quakers were cruelly persecuted, the Mormons scourged across the continent and forbidden to worship God according to the dictates of their own conscience even in the western wilderness. We boycott in business and politics such agnostics as presume to criticize our creed, defame deists, and compel Jew and Gentile to observe our Sabbath or go to jail; yet we hold up our hands in holy horror if the followers of Buddha and Allah do not receive our missionaries with open arms and feed them on the fat of the land!

The Monroe Doctrine

The Monroe Doctrine, literally interpreted, is simply a warning to transatlantic powers to keep off the American grass.

N

Nature

Nature plays no favorites. When she gives a man a lower-case brain she makes amends by supplying him with a display-type mouth.

• • • • •

Warm sunlight and wet water prove that nothing is impossible in nature.

The New Woman

When I reflect that until comparatively recent times women were slaves, I don't wonder that the old civilizations went to the dogs.

• • • • •

For ages woman was but man's plaything, her occupation the amusement of his idle hours—valuable chiefly for breeding purposes. The highest educational advantages were denied her, the professions closed against her as an incapable. Her talents were supposed to be small, and little opportunity was offered for their enlargement... [The New Woman] is simply a hard-sensed young lady who politely but pointedly declines to play second fiddle in the great diapason of humanity—to be bound by the foolish fashions and inept customs that have cursed her sex for sixty centuries. She does not object to matrimony, but declines to regard the capture of some sapheaded dude with a few dollars as the end and aim of her existence.... Her ideals of wifehood and motherhood are too exalted to permit her sitting supinely down on the matrimonial block, like Patience on a monument, and waiting for some bumptious he-thing to straddle along who will consent to supply her with board and clothes—in consideration of the surrender of her freedom and the debauchment of her beauty. She prefers to gird up her patent health corset and go out into the world to hustle her own hash.

• • • • •

Cleopatra drank pearls dissolved in wine, but whiskey straight is said to be good enough for some of her successors.

• • • • •

Too many young ladies rush into literature instead of the laundry, become poets of passion instead of authors of pie.

• • • • •

The New Woman is certainly getting there. Her costume is mannish, she can swallow four fingers of red licker without blinking, has taken to real tobacco cigarettes, and expects soon to be able to expectorate without craning her neck and to scratch a match on the seat of her pants.

A Newspaper Recipe

Here is the recipe for making a "great daily"; let them who have stomachs for such work apply themselves: a scandal-in-high-life, first-page, double-leaded, screamer-head; two or three columns of rocking chair speculation on matters political, Washington date lines; a few bogus or garbled interviews with prominent politicians; a suicide; a scandal-in-low-life; a thrilling account of an impossible accident in Timbuctoo; report that a billion Chinese have been drowned by an overflow of the Hwang-Ho; full and circumstantial report of a sensational divorce trial—not intended for Sunday-school reading; two column account of a prize fight; a hanging, with all the ghastly details "worked up"; two columns of esoteric baseball lingo in which the doughty deeds of "Fatty," "Shorty," "Squatty," "Bow-legged Bill" and "Short-stop Sam" are painted in wonderful chiar-oscuro; account of the elopement of a society belle with a negro coachman; heavy editorial on the "Power of the Press"; more editorial inanity and offensive self-glorification; a pimping "personal" column; two columns of murdered men and English language; more toothsome scandal; market reports to mislead the country merchant; budget of foreign news—manufactured in New York; interesting case of ministerial crim. con.; advertisements of quack doctors, lost manhood restorers, syphilitic nostrums, preventative pills, and other things calculated to set the cheek of modesty aflame; local miscellany; police court reports and taffy in solid slugs. Jam to a mux and serve hot. Price, 5 cents. Now is the time to subscribe.

Newspapers: The American Press

Truthful as a Cretin! Courageous as Falstaff! Independent as Uriah Heep!

• • • • •

Men do not establish daily newspapers for the express purpose of reforming the world, but rather to print what a large number of people desire to read and are willing to pay for.

• • • • •

The press is the public educator, the Archimedean lever that moves the world—to retch itself into spasms.

• • • • •

There was a time when the principal business of the American Press was the publication of important news and the expression of opinion anent matters of moment. In those days it posed as a "public educator," and the self-bestowed title was not altogether inappropriate; but it has, for the most part, dropped its high pretensions and is now notoriously "out for the stuff."

• • • • •

A clean active newsgatherer is a blessing to any community. It is a great comfort to be informed betimes whether John Smith is getting wived or shrived, hanged or only elevated to office. We like to know when the Hon. Wilyum Shaw harvests his hoop-poles and when Col. Hogg Uncorks himself on the canal question; whether Grant or Green will be permitted to name the postmaster at Podunk. We want to laugh with those who laugh, weep with those who weep, and drink with all the candidates.

• • • • •

What is the American newspaper that it should pose as a regulator-in-general of the universe? It is a combination of gossip-monger and political propagandist. The old woman peddling tittle-tattle or exploring scandal over her back-fence and seasoning it to suit the palate of her auditors, is doing free-gratis exactly what the "great daily" does for so much per annum. Its mission is not to eradicate prejudices and emolliate animosities, but to inflame and fatten on them; to "elucidate great and vital questions," but to act as special pleader for some hungry political faction with a view to pecuniary profit.

• • • • •

I may be somewhat archaic in my ideas, but I hold to the theory that the mainstay of a paper should be its readers instead of its advertising acreage.

• • • • •

Let me tell you that every success this country has witnessed during the past three decades has been achieved despite the morning press.

• • • • •

They know that should they print the grandest sermon that ever fell from Massillon's lips of gold, not 20 percent, even of the professedly pious, would read it; but that a detailed account of a fragrant divorce case or international prizefight will cause 99 percent of the very elect of the Lord to swoop down upon it like a hungry hen-hawk on an unripe gosling and fairly devour it, then roll their eyes to heaven like a calf with the colic and wonder what this wicked old world is coming to.

• • • • •

The daily newspaper unquestionably has its use, but about eight days in a week it is an insufferable dam-nuisance. A man may get himself covered with honor an inch thick and have gilt-edge glory plastered on him with a trowel, and the chances are that the newspapers will never notice him, or if they do will accord him a three-line paragraph tucked away among the ads; but let him be accused of some heinous crime, or his wife be caught philandering with some other fellow, and forthwith he is given a front-page "spread" with headlines that would scare a cable-car.

• • • • •

The would-be great morning dailies are evidently striving to outdo each other in journalistic idiocy. Their Sunday editions, especially, are fearfully and wonderfully made. Some of those issued by New York and Chicago publishers are about the size of the U.S. Census Report, and their component parts are "want ads," cheap woodcuts, and wind. They have now taken to colored illustrations and resemble nothing so much as painted bladders blown to the bursting point.

• • • • •

When a newspaper tells the truth, even by accident, it should stick with it.

O

Oklahoma

Some time ago in paying my respects to Kansas, the home of Prohibition cranks and she-make politicians, I intimated that Nebraska was one hind leg of the eastbound earth and Oklahoma the other, and now the fair editress of the *Enid Wave* is protesting lustily against the position assigned that fruitful land. I am perfectly willing to make Kansas one hind leg of the earth animal and Texas the other, if the angry lady would be better pleased with the new location.

The Optimist

The optimist is a good gift, for which we should be grateful. He is the brass band in the political procession, the Hallelujah at the Methodist camp meeting. Overtaken by the deluge, he would not drown, but, like a champagne cork, bob serenely to the surface of that circumambient sea. Were old Sol to go out of business, he would proclaim it a blessing and prove it with sunstroke statistics—would insist that enough light and heat could be extracted from our stock of canned cucumbers until time shall be no more.

P

Patriotism

Patriotism has been throttled by greed, fraternity by jealousy. We no longer send our best men to Congress. We do not ask what a candidate can do to make the Union stronger; we do not inquire what he knows of the science of government—but rather how deep a haul he can make on the treasury for the special behoof of our section; how large an appropriation he can secure for the "improvement" of intermittent creeks and impossible harbors; how many fat federal offices he can distribute among us. We are after the spoils; we have made of our votes levers to pry open the public treasury; we will follow any demogogue if he but lead us to the fleshpots, reckless of the future.

Poets & Poetry

People really suffering for pills imagine themselves pregnant with poems—mistake a torrid liver for divine afflatus.

• • • • •

Poets? We've got 'em; got 'em in flocks, swarms, droves and shoals—got 'em to burn, perhaps. The population of America is 73 million people—72 million poets, the rest Populists. The Homeric era and Elizabethan Age have become mere grease spots on the robes of the gods. Poems are manufactured to order while you wait. Drop a nickel in the slot and get a tune—sonnet, ode, or elegy. Great is science.

• • • • •

Carlyle ranges like an archangel through the universe of intellect, overturning mountains to see how they are made.

• • • • •

Tennyson is the Sir Galahad of poets. His song, while seldom cold, is ever chaste as ice. To turn from Byron to Tennyson is like passing from a drunken revel with nymphs *du pavé* into the society of vestal virgins.

Politics & Politicians

What's a platform for but to get in on?

• • • • •

Perhaps it never occurred to you that the average Congressman costs this country some $15,000 per annum, exclusive of the incidental damage he does.

• • • • •

Muttonheads are called to the chief places of honor simply because the masses can understand and appreciate mediocrity.

• • • • •

As soon as Little Boy Blue learns to blow his horn he wants to ride on the bandwagon.

• • • • •

I have noticed that, as a rule, the less a man knows of the science of government the crazier he is to go to Congress.

• • • • •

We have fallen upon the bad habit of making our higher offices into an old folks' refuge or asylum for senility, sending to the lower house of Congress pettifogging attorneys who cannot pick up a livelihood by practice in the chicken courts.

The U.S. Postal Service

Under our blessed democratic "reform" administration, Uncle Sam's postal service is the most utterly unreliable and shamefully inefficient to be found on the face of the earth.

• • • • •

When a man lacks sufficient judgment to manage a mule, and cannot be trusted in a cotton patch without a keeper, he secures a situation in the postal service.

• • • • •

If Uncle Sam should assume control of the railways and manage them as he does the paper mail, the trains would wander off into the woods, and it would be necessary to send out tracers to discover the whereabouts of lost depots.

Poverty

Know Ye not that the poorest beggar is an earth-passenger also?

• • • • •

Hungry men are always dangerous—no man can be a patriot on an empty stomach.

• • • • •

Do you know that it is more dangerous for a beggar to steal a mule than for a plutocrat to kill a man?

• • • • •

When I think of three thousand children in the single city of Chicago without rags to shield their nakedness from the keen north wind; of the ten thousand innocents, such as Christ blessed, who die in New York every year of the world for lack of food; of the millions in every country whose cries go up night and day to God's great throne—not for salvation, but for soup; not the robe of righteousness, but for a secondhand pair of pants—and then contemplate those beside whose hoarded wealth the riches of Lydia's ancient kings were but a beggar's patrimony, praying to Him who reversed the law of nature to feed the poor, I long for the mystic power to coin sentences that sear like sulphur flames come hot from hell, and weave of words a whip of scorpions to lash the rascals naked through the world.

Prayer

Certainly, you should give thanks to God, for, however deplorable your condition, it is doubtless better than you deserve.

• • • • •

Down upon thy knees, aspiring pigmy, and give thanks to God thou wast not born a beast—that the best of terrestrial life is thine, with the joys of infancy, the pride of manhood, and the halo of age. Take the good the gods provide and hold thy peace. If it be Heaven's will that a happier world awaits thee beyond the tomb's pale portals, rejoice that thou art rewarded beyond thy desserts; if not, lie down like a tired child upon its mother's breast, and pass without a sign into the eternal, the imperishable elements from which thou wert called—back into the great Life Ocean that is God.

• • • • •

You were not sent hither to spend your time on your knees, else God had not given you feet.

• • • • •

(Written to a complaining minister)

Pray for me? And to whom? To the ignorant Deity you adore—simply because he's an idealization of yourself? Well, don't let me catch you in the act; that's all! Your God is not my God. Your great What-is-it has prepared for the sons of men one bad place which you name Hell, and a worse you call Heaven. May the All-merciful Father of the human brotherhood preserve me from both!

A Prayer Challenge

Solely in the interest of truth, I propose to make a test of this "direct visitation in answer to prayer" hypothesis; to subject it to the *experimentum crucis,* that the fraud may be exposed if it is a fraud, and the fact forever established if it is a fact. To this end I ask the earnest cooperation of Christians of every sect who believe in the physical power of prayer—who hold that the plans of the Omnipotent ever were or ever will be altered by the supplication of any mortal son of Adam's misery. I ask all such to pray earnestly, night and morning from now until February 1, next, that I will drop dead at exactly noon that day. If your prayer is answered, atheism will be practically obliterated, the scoffer would fall upon his knees and confess the glory of God. Thousands of men and women who were better than I can ever hope to be . . . have gladly died that others might believe, and inherit the joys of Heaven; but never yet did the loss of a single life contribute so much to the propagation of the Christian faith as would my removal by the power of prayer in the very noonday of this Age of Denial. Nor is this all: the pulpiteers frequently accuse me of "poisoning the minds of the people." If this be true I richly deserve a speedy death. I am not defying the Deity. Why should I? If He exists, were I not an ass to challenge omnipotence? I stake my earthly existence on the simple proposition that Infinite Wisdom will not suffer itself to be guided by finite folly. I do not defy the Deity, but I do defy the entire world to pray the nail off my little finger. The assumption that Jehovah is kept on the jump—like a hen on a hot griddle—by petitions that he change his administrative policy, belittles and belies him, is either the folly of barbarisms or deliberate blasphemy. The man who presumes to tender advice to Almighty God should be given a hot mush poultice for his gall. I am of the opinion that there are no "direct visitations" in answer to prayer.

A Prayer for the Reverend Mister Tally

Almighty Creator of the Universe—Jehovah or Jove, Brahma or Buddha—dear Father of all men, of whatsoever faith; be good, I prithee, to Tally, my erring brother. Hadst thou intended that he would be wise thou wouldst have built his head for a bigger hat. Thou, who didst evolve the molecules from primordial matter and build the industrious doodlebug, called the spirit of Tally from the great inane and gave it a habitation and a name. He is thy handiwork, O God, not mine. . . . Father, forgive him. . . . If it not be inconsistent with thy great plan, broaden his intellect until he can comprehend that not every man destitute of the Baptist watermark is slipping dynamite bombs under thy throne of dazzling brightness. Make him to understand that the world rolled on for countless ages, through joy and through sorrow, through glory and through shame, before a single "locus" preacher of the Baptist persuasion crawled from Time's fecund womb to supervise its future. Thou can'st teach him, if thou wilt, that the finite has no power to harm infinity. Thou can'st, by building his head anew, and refurnishing it throughout, make him understand that we are but a breed of moths, flitting through the light of one brief day, between a night that had no beginning and that can have no end; that thou dost not sit secure in some far citadel issuing baptismal ordinances from a mystic cloud, while unfeathered bipeds dance a holy can-can and indulge in one everlasting grand opera; but liv'st in all that is, or was, or ever can be, from the smallest monadic Tally to the mightiest Shakespearean Titan. Yea, God, thou can'st do this—but not without creating an immediate vacancy in the sectarian ministry.

Preachers

A whale swallowed one Jonah, then puked him up in disgust on learning that he had a call to preach.

• • • • •

I haven't much use for gold-plated godliness. Christ never built a church, or asked for a vacation on full pay—never.

• • • • •

Men who have managed in some mysterious manner to dodge the madhouse, believe that priests or preachers are the special deputies of the Deity, that a criticism of the clergy is an insult to the Almighty—that if you dare dissent from the foolish opinions of some woodenheaded *dominus* anent the Divine Plan you might as well "curse God and die."

• • • • •

There are ministers occupying prominent Texas pulpits who haven't originated an idea in forty years, and who would not recognize the Incarnate Son of God if they met him in the road. It is not necessary that a man should possess an iota or intellect to become a popular preacher. In fact, brains are but in his way, for in orthodoxy there is absolutely no room for reason. Let him but select the heavenly turnpike on which he suspects there will be the most travel, set up his little tollgate, and he'll soon have a mob of sanctified nonentities about him who shame the Devil at his own game on weekdays and try to bunco the blessed Saviour on Sunday.

• • • • •

Having obtained the ascendancy over a number of ignorant fanatics, the small-town preacher is practically master of the situation, the lord high executioner of the community, for the business and professional element, from the barber's clerk to the candidate for Congress, is largely dependent upon the patronage of these dupes. It becomes, according to the unwritten law of the community, a greater crime to criticize the clergyman than to commit a homicide or steal a horse.

• • • • •

People who couldn't be trusted to wean a calf tell us all about the Creator of the Cosmos.

• • • • •

I am not warring upon religious faith but on those who mistake bile for benevolence, gall for godliness, and chronic laziness for "a call to preach."

• • • • •

There are a great many grand and noble ministers but there also are too many hacking 'round with their little hoes in the Lord's Vineyard who could do more effective work in the cotton patch—or the penitentiary.

• • • • •

The public appears amply able to take care of itself—it has put more than a thousand preachers in the penitentiary.

• • • • •

There was never a religion instituted upon this earth that the priest had failed to transform into errant folly, or debase until it finally fell into disrepute.

O dammit!

• • • • •

The Lord never yet "called" a preacher to serve for a smaller salary.

• • • • •

At the opposite extreme we find blatant blackguardism by so-called evangelists, who were educated in a mulepen and dismissed without a diploma, yet who set up as instructors of the masses in the profound mysteries of the Almighty. Men who would get shipwrecked in the poetry of Shakespeare, or lost in the philosophy of one of his fools, pretend to interpret the plans of Him who writes His thoughts in flaming words on the papyri of immensity, whose sentences are astral fire.

• • • • •

Of course, every man's an atheist who doesn't see God through Deacon Twogood's telescope, and every man a blasphemer who applies historical criticism to the Bible— who attempts to separate the word of God from the folly of the redactors.

• • • • •

I regard with unspeakable contempt those men who decry all religious progress and brand as blasphemers those would take one step beyond the crude faiths of former days, insist that religion is too sacred to be handled by human reason.

• • • • •

Rev. Wm. Goodrich, a Baptist preacher occupying a Kansas pulpit, is being subjected to much adverse criticism. He declared that he "could do better work for God and humanity" if unsexed, and voluntarily submitted to the surgeon. I am inclined to think that he is correct in his premise—that it would be a good idea to unsex all apostles of emotional piety. They may not thenceforth be quite so popular with the super-sanctified sisters who mistake the minister for the Almighty, but they will enjoy the confidence of the male members of the community.

Presidents

We have been making presidents of scrub stock entirely too long.

• • • • •

Presidents save seven-figure fortunes on five-figure salaries and are applauded by people who profess to be respectable.

• • • • •

We cannot transform a porker into a philosopher by calling it Plato, nor make a statesman of a tub of offal by electing it President.

The Professions

Entirely too many youngsters are rushing into the professions instead of the cornfield. Lawyers and preachers, doctors and dentists are being ground out by the thousands—and two-thirds of those already at large in the land have nothing in their pockets but an elegant assortment of holes. The woods are full of barristers without briefs, preachers without pulpits, and physicians without patients.

Prohibition & Prohibitionists

The Prohibitionist, like the cutworm and the financial crank, is again abroad in the land. When in that happier world beyond the skies, we are permitted to praise God without pausing for meals, we will probably learn why he has elected to plague us with thorns and thistles, pismires and Prohibitionists.

• • • • •

The Prohibs probably mean well; but they are incapable of learning, even in the school of experience, that just so long as whiskey is made it will be drunk—that Prohibition means simply a poor brand of booze.

O dammit!

• • • • •

You may prove five hundred different religious dogmas by the Bible, but Prohibition is not one of them. Bro. [William] Homan declares that the Old Testament prohibits the drinking of wine. It does not; but it does make circumcision obligatory.

• • • • •

Some of you Prohibs don't know who Narcissus was. Well, he was one of those fellows whom cold water killed.

• • • • •

Water is an indispensable, but too much of it once wrecked the world.

• • • • •

Mixing religion and politics is like mixing whiskey and water—it spoils both.

• • • • •

Christ turned water into wine at the wedding feast, when He could just as easily have made Hostetter's Bitters or some other popular Prohibition beverage. It was wine and of the best—perhaps Mumm's Extra Dry. Were our dear Lord on earth today He would be more liable to transform artesian water into Anheuser-Busch or Kentucky cocktails than to paddle about the whining Prohibitionists.

• • • • •

There is no more reason why we should banish whiskey and beer because some are drunkards than that we should banish meat and bread because some are gluttons. Some men commit crimes when under the influence of liquor, but more because of women or greed for gold. Now if we banish liquor because it encourages crime, we should, to be consistent, send all the wealth and women with it—and if the ladies don't object, I'll go along. Some men go crazy because of "red-eye" but more because of religion. Shall we, therefore, knock in the heads of our barrels and burn our Bibles? If there were no liquor there would be no drunkards, and if there were no wealth there would be no robbers. If there were no food there'd be no gourmands, and if there were no offices there'd be no Jim Crow politicians. If there were no water, nobody would be drowned.

• • • • •

I regard the saloon much as I do the undertaking establishment. Man will drink and man will die. No law ever devised by human brain has banished drunkenness or abolished death.

• • • • •

It is common knowledge that the Lord kept that old sot, Noah, for seed, while letting the Prohibitionists drown.

• • • • •

Go ahead, gentlemen: make Waco a dry town and give the jug dealers and Dallas dealers a chance. Shut up the decent saloon and inaugurate the disreputable "blind-tiger"—where the most villainous varieties of coffin paint are passed out by a hidden hand at the same old price. Compel us to import our beer and ice it at home—the bottles will make handy playthings for the babies, and serve to remind them that their fathers are not freemen. Waco will then be such a nice quiet resort for overworked people from Dallas and Fort Worth when they want complete rest, and the grass in our streets will make a charming refuge for the mule-eared rabbit. With the saloon hermetically sealed—at one end, at least—we can then turn our attention to forms of baptism, take water in all styles, and live upon one another as cozily and comfortably as a basket of adders.

Protestantism

Protestantism is today little more than an army of generals, its supposed strength but the populace attracted by their gaudy uniforms and the music of its mercenaries.

• • • • •

The Protestants of every sect oppress and persecute just as far as they possess the power.

• • • • •

Call up the editors and reporters of this country and they will tell you that the Catholic priests and Jewish Rabbis meddle with their work but little; but that, with the possible exceptions of the pothouse politicians and crank scribblers, the Protestant clergy is the greatest nuisance with which they have to deal.

Public Opinion

A law cannot be enforced that is not steadily upheld by public opinion.

• • • • •

It is a difference of opinion that keeps the world from going to the dogs. Independence of thought, nought of accepted dogmas, the spirit of inquiry, the desire to know—is the mighty lever that has lifted man so far above the brute level.

• • • • •

When the pendulum swings too far in one direction, it is sure to swing too far in the other.

Pugilism

State Senator Morriss of Texas wants to make the exhibition of prizefight pictures punishable by ten years in the pen. He is a mighty reformer, is State Senator Morriss, and is determined that the blessed people shall not be permitted to look upon anything brutalizing. When he gets prizefight pictures suppressed he will eliminate from all family Bibles Dore's portraits of Samson's "go" with the Philistines, the wrestling match between Jacob and the angel, and the rattling mill between David and Goliath. Senator Morriss hath a great head—but he ought to wear a thimble over it lest some marauding bluejay mistake it for an acorn.

Q

Queen Victoria's Golden Jubilee

I did not accept the Queen's invitation to attend her Diamond Jubilee, my cotton being badly in the grass and the bollworm hard at work; but I think Vic will understand that I meant no offense by remaining with my roan mule and cultivator instead of occupying a seat in her carriage, helping entertain the crowd, and slinging a little *éclat* into the occasion. I notice that she succeeded in pulling her Jubilee off without my assistance. Vic's a gay old girl who knows how to give an A-1 show without going into her sock for a shilling. Of course, it was nothing like the Waco carnival, still it did very well for London.

R

Reform and Revolution

The "radical reformer" is not satisfied with saving less than the world. The "conservative" is satisfied if he can save the particular portion of it in which he resides.

• • • • •

We boast of progress? Progress whither? From the slavery of the auction block and cat-o'-nine-tails to that of the great industrial system, where souls as well as bodies are bought and sold, while thousands and tens of thousands beg in God's great name for the poor privilege of wearing out their wretched lives in the brutal treadmill.

• • • • •

Lead a successful revolt and you're a pure patriot whose memory should be preserved to latest posterity; head an unsuccessful upstaging and you're a miserable rebel who should have been hanged.

Religion

O Religion, how much d——d dirty deadbeatism is perpetrated in thy name!

• • • • •

If in the wilds of Central Africa I should find a man bowing down to a dried toad, a stuffed snake, I'd remove my hat as a tribute of respect, not to his judgment, but to his honesty.

• • • • •

A cult is simply an expression, more or less crude, of the religious sentiment of a people, the poor garment with which finite man clothes infinity.

• • • • •

From the standpoint of a statesman, it makes little difference what the religion of a people may be so long as most of them believe it.

• • • • •

I have ever held to the theory that the man who must be convinced by cold logic of God's existence is a spiritual wreck scarce worth the salvage; that religion, like poetry and song, art and eloquence, must be born with a man and cannot be driven into him later with a maul—that it depends, not so much upon fallible human reason as upon a subtler sense which puts the finite in touch with the infinitude, is a constant testimony, a perennial revelation.

• • • • •

Religion is the poetry of the common people.

• • • • •

The oldest gods of Greece were borrowed.

• • • • •

Every religious cult has miracles in plenty and martyrs galore—the first all falsehood, the latter mostly fools.

• • • • •

It is a sad commentary upon all religious faiths that they flourish best where ignorance prevails.

• • • • •

Cult wars with cult, and sect with sect, while all unite to damn the independent worshiper; yet every man who bows the knee or breathes a prayer to any God of whatsoever name; every Egyptian bending at Isis's fanes, and every Phoenician sacrificing unto Baal; every Gueber worshipping his god of fire, and every Catholic following the sacred cross; every Peruvian adoring the rising sun, and every

Methodist agonizing at the mourner's bench, is a member of the same great church. They may accredit their God with different attributes and worship him in diverse ways, but their faiths, when stripped of nonessentials, are one and the same—their Deities are identical.

• • • • •

Why quarrel about our faiths, and declare that this is right or that wrong, when all religions are, and must of necessity ever be, fundamentally one and the same—the worship of a Superior Power.

• • • • •

Religion is becoming little more than a luxury, the temple a sumptuous palace wherein people ennuied with themselves may parade their costly clothes, have their jaded passions soothed by sensuous music, their greed for the bizarre satiated by sensational sermons.

• • • • •

I have great respect for true religion; but for the brand of holiness that's put on with the Sunday shirt—that makes a man cry ahmen with unction, but doesn't prevent him selling five- and ten-cent cigars out of the same box, oleomargarine and creamery butter out of the same bucket, benzene and bourbon whiskey out of the same barrel, which makes long prayers on Sunday and gives short weights on Monday, which worries about the welfare of good-looking young women, but gives the old grandames the go-by, which fathers the orphan only if he's rich and husbands the widow only if she's handsome, is an errant Humbug, a crime against man, an offense to God.

• • • • •

It does not follow because some church communicants are hypocrites that all religion is a humbug; that because the Bible winks at incest and robbery, murder and slavery, the book is but a tissue of foolish falsehoods; that because Almighty God has not seen proper to reveal Himself in all His supernal splendor to Messrs. Hume and Voltaire, Paine and Ingersoll, the world has no good reason for belief in his existence.

• • • • •

The core of all religion is the worship of a Supreme Power, and the belief in man's immortality. That is the central idea, around which the imagination of man has woven many a complicated web, some beautiful as Arachne's robe, some barbaric and repulsive, but all of little worth. The wise man, the true philosopher, will not mistake the machinery of a religion for the religious idea, the garment which ignorance weaves for Omniscience, for God himself.

• • • • •

Perhaps I am not strictly orthodox. I have an idea that the religion which does not sink clear down to the hypogastric region of a man's soul and mold or modify his daily life, that doesn't eliminate his animal nature and make him gentle and pure and honest to the heart's core, is of little use as a Delmonico meal ticket to a starving pilgrim in the Sahara desert.

• • • • •

There is no necessary relationship between morality and religion.

• • • • •

Had the Christian religion failed to take root, Judas Iscariot would have been commemorated in the archives of Rome as one who helped stamp out the heresy.

• • • • •

Yet we assume that Almighty God, who hung the midnight heaven with patines of pure gold and painted the rings of Saturn—that even he, Architect of the Universe—left his eternal throne, star-gemmed, canopied with clouds of incense upon which ever falls the bright effulgence of solar systems, through which rolls the eternal melody of the spheres, came down to earth and of the cold dead clay made a miserable biped and called it his masterpiece; that he is now following it about with notebook, jotting down the inconsequential doings of this miserable microbe—observing with jealous solicitude how it is baptized, what the "article" of its religion, whether it worships as Buddhist or Baptist, Methodist or Mormon!

Religion & Politics

Our States are practically theocracies, our legislatures ecumenical councils by which those religious dogmas entertained by the majority are declared the law of the land and enforced by judicial process, the posse comitatus and the entire military force at the command of the government.

• • • • •

Whenever I see a sanctified yap who is short on brains and long on gall standing up in the Texas legislature and unwinding a two-minute perfunctory prayer for a $5 bill which I must help to pay, I feel less kindly to his creed and all his class. When I am denied a bath, a shave, or a glass of beer on Sunday because my enjoyment thereof would give a job lot of whining pietists a pain, I conclude that if God interests himself in such bigots he's in precious small business. When I hear it urged against a candidate for office that he's a Catholic or Atheist, I instinctively reach for a stuffed club.

• • • • •

I care never a copper whether a man takes his theology from the Pope or Dalai Lama, John Calvin or Joseph Smith, so long as he doesn't persist in mixing it with American politics.

• • • • •

I do protest that when a preacher invites people to hear him discourse of the beauties of religion, then regales them with a disquisition on partisan politics and an indecent exposure of his economical ignorance, he should be seized tenderly but firmly by the bust of his panties and "trun tro de roof." There may be preachers who know something about politics; there may be ministers who have made an exhaustive study of economics; but during forty years wandering in this terrestrial wilderness I failed to find 'em.

• • • • •

The modern preacher is going extensively into politics—is devoting fully as much time and attention to party platforms as to the Prince of Peace. The churches are being transformed into political wigwams where the people are taught, not how to save their souls, but how to save the country—are instructed in the esoteric science of economics by men who could scarce tell a customhouse receipt from a kangaroo ballot.

Religious Intolerance & Persecution

Do not take it for granted that whatever pleases the people originated in perdition.

• • • • •

True piety does not consist in preventing other people enjoying themselves.

• • • • •

Too many people presume that they are full of the grace of God when they're only bilious; that they are pious because they dislike to see other people enjoy themselves; that they are Christians because they conform to certain creeds, just as many men imagine themselves honest because they obey the laws of the land—for the purpose of keeping out of the penitentiary.

• • • • •

Were the Presbyterians, Methodists, and Baptists so powerful in America as the Catholics in Spain, I'd get a touch of the Inquisition before I was many hours older. Jews and Catholics would have to recant or leave the country. We'd have an established church, a test act, and other unpleasant reminders of "Reformation" times. Were the Atheists all-powerful, a man could not publicly worship God without being informed that he was a superstitious idiot and otherwise insulted.

• • • • •

Fortunately the liberal element dominates in Texas, as it does in every civilized country, and the fiendish wolf of fanaticism can only tug at its chain and show its venomous teeth. Not being permitted to put men and women to the torture for uttering their honest convictions in a land of so-called religious liberty; to flay them alive for daring to dissent from some ridiculous dogma cooked up by half-crazed dunderheads during the Dark Ages; to drag them at cart's tail and bore their tongues with hot irons in the name of a beneficent Deity, these professed followers of the Man of Galilee resort to sneaking boycotts, petty annoyances, and cowardly calumnies. They prove in every way possible that their hearts, instead of being full to overflowing with the grace of God and the catholic charity of Christ, are bitter little pools in whose poisonous waters and fetid scum writhe and wriggle unclean reptiles such as Dante saw in the desolate regions of the damned.

• • • • •

"Thou shalt" and "Thou shalt not" are scorpion whips that goad the sons of men to mutiny.

• • • • •

A soul is an immaterial thing. You cannot flay it with aspic's fangs nor kerosene it and set it on fire.

• • • • •

It would be a misfortune should supreme political power pass into the hands of any particular religious cult. Were Protestantism united, instead of divided into dozens of warring factions, every freethinker would be hanged before nightfall.

• • • • •

The New England Puritans who hanged witches and persecuted Quakers felt that they were discharging a disagreeable duty. They were the creatures of an ignorant and superstitious but God-fearing age, and their cruelties were performed more in sorrow than in anger. With them religion was a serious thing and morality its synonym. If ignorant they were honest, and if brutal they were brave.

• • • • •

It is not strange that religionists should invade the private rights and civic prerogatives of those who dare differ with them, when they read in holy writ that such offenders are deserving of death.

• • • • •

Let it be said of a man that he is an infidel—that he does not swallow, unquestioned, every draught prepared by preachers, does not accept as literally true every thing found between the lids of the Bible. And the ministry, instead of attempting by kindly arguments to convince him that he is in error, begins a bitter war of denunciation and misrepresentations, opens the sluice-gates of its vindictive hatred, deluges him with a torrent of "Christian" calumny!

• • • • •

The Deist, the Atheist, and the Agnostic have no political rights which the Religionists feel bound to respect.

• • • • •

Were it possible for religious intolerance to destroy a nation, Columbia would soon pass from the map of the world, for in all God's universe there is not another so cursed with stupid bigotry and intolerant bile. If a man is a Catholic the Protestants want to disfranchise him; if a Jew he is compelled under pains and penalties to observe as the Sabbath a day which he does not consider sacred; if an Atheist he is ostracized politically and boycotted commercially; if a Deist he is between the devil and the deep sea, a target for the shafts of everybody, for the Christians fear him more than they do the Atheist, while the Atheists regard him as the Hector of Superstition's stronghold. And this is "the land of religious liberty!"

Religion & Patent Medicine

I opine that no paper exploiting the proprietary remedies ... has an idea of alleviating the miseries of mankind. Every editor who can distinguish between a man and woman without a diagram knows full well that ninety-and-nine percent of those nostrums are frauds, and oftentimes more dangerous than disease. The papers that accept such advertisements have simply gone into partnership with quacks for the express purpose of fleecing the public.

O dammit!

• • • • •

There are many things of which I would speak to you; but what lies heaviest on my heart is the fact that most if not all the religious contemporaries of *The Iconoclast* are in the habit of ladling out saving grace with one hand while raking in the shekels with the other for flaming advertisements of syphilitic nostrums, "lost manhood" restorers, and kindred quack remedies for diseases with which the faithful are supposed to be unfamiliar. It grieves me to note that the purveyors of "panaceas" for private diseases regard the religious press as the best possible medium of reaching prospective patrons. It doth grieve the Apostle sore to see his brother ministers acting as bell-ringers for quack doctors and assiduously shoving degrading advertisements into the faces of decent people, regardless of age or sex. It shocks his sense of proprieties to see a great religious journal like the *Texas Baptist Standard* flaunting in the middle of a page of jejune prattle anent the Holy Spirit, a big display ad. for the "French Nerve Pill"—guaranteed to re-stallionize old *roués*—and following up a long dissertation on "The Weakness of the Baptist Denomination" with an illustrated notice to the effect that "loss of manly power resulting from bad habits" is cured by certain eastern Cagliostros, who will send "securely sealed in plain envelope on receipt of ten cents" a medical treatise "written in plain language." Perhaps the Apostle is entirely too sensitive where the reputation of his brethren in Christ is concerned; but it does grate upon his nerves to see a really good sermon in the *Texas Baptist* and *Herald* flanked by an advertisement of "Pennyroyal Pills"—especially designed to produce abortions!

• • • • •

It does seem that we publishers of religious papers who pray frequently and preach occasionally; who bellyache about blasphemers whenever a scholar presumes to apply historical criticism to the Bible; who insist that we have been divinely ordained to preach a living morality to a dying world; who have discovered the only sure road to the Celestial City, and erected tollgates thereon, should make a reasonable effort to be decent as well as devout.

• • • • •

Among the quarter million readers of *The Iconoclast,* but two or three cases of "lost manhood" have developed, and the patients immediately stopped their paper.

Royalty

Genuine French noblemen can always find employment. They make the best of barbers, the most obsequious of waiters, while as cooks they defy competition.

• • • • •

Strange that when an American family amasses a little money by boring for oil, boiling soap, or trading in toothpicks and tripe, it at once begins snuffing about the boots of the European nobility.

• • • • •

The titled European is usually some down-at-the-heels dude who must find a wife capable of supporting him, else go to work. Some prosperous American pork-packer or soap-boiler buys him, just as he would purchase a collie dog, and gives him to a gangle-shanked, putty-faced daughter whom no self-respecting he-American would have.

• • • • •

The fact that the *parvenus* are paying fancy prices for coats-of-arms suggests that we might discharge the national debt by amending the constitution so as to permit the president to sell patents of nobility after the manner of the mediaeval princes. Our prosperous hog morgue manager would give half their holdings to be "ennobled." By all means, let us have a few Barons d'Brewery and Earls d'Oleomargarine, Laundry Soap Lords and Packing House Princes. They would gladly bear all governmental burdens for the privilege of playing the fool.

The Russians

A Russian peasant smells like the Chicago River on a summer's day. He will eat what would send a coyote howling out of the country. To him a jug of train oil were as angel food, a keg of stale soap grease a feral feast. During his entire life he enjoys but two baths—one when he is born, the other when he's buried. Doubtless the rule of the bayonet is the only government possible for such a barbarous people—and the Romanoffs have not allowed it to rust.

• • • • •

[Nicholas II] is emphatically an emperor who emps. He isn't bothered with do-nothing Congresses or Populist politicians who want him impeached. When he saith to a man "Come," he cometh, p.d.q.; to another "go," he getteth a hustle on him that would shame a pneumatic tire. With more barbaric mummery, flummery, and vulgar waste of wealth than characterized even the late Marlborough-Vanderbilt wedding, Nicholas Two-Eyes was crowned Emperor of the ragtag and bobtail of creation, officially known as "all the Russias." Nick has a nice easy job at a salary considerably in excess of ye average country editor, and he gets it all in gold rubles instead of post-oak cordwood and green watermelons.

S

The Sacred Books

There never was an atheistical book written, there was never an infidel argument penned, that touched the core of any religion, Christian or pagan. Bibles, Korans, Zend-Avestas—all sacred books—are but the feeble effort of finite man to interpret the Infinite, to speak forth the unspeakable, to reduce to intelligible human characters the flame-written hieroglyphs of the sky.

San Antonio

The National Convention of the T.P.A. [Travelers' Protective Association of America] will be held this month in San Antonio, the metropolis of Texas, the most interesting city on the American continent. The "boys" will fall in love with San Antonio, because, like themselves, it is broad-gauged, hospitable, little addicted to the vice of hypocrisy. Many of them who come from the older States will probably expect to find a wild and woolly frontier town, where bad whiskey's four bits a drink and the festive cowboy chases the elusive Longhorn through the principal streets, shoots out the kerosene streetlamps, rides his bronco up to the bar when yearning for a compound of tarantula juice and creosote; to be met at the train by a deputation of leading citizens who wear their pants in their boots and boycott their barbers, and welcomed by Mayor Elmendorf from the hurricane deck of a cayuse. But those expecting to "rough it" will be happily disappointed. They will find a cultured city possessing all the modern improvements, including a municipal debt—a grand old commonwealth gleaming in the glorious sunlight of West Texas, a jewel pendant from the fringe of Civilization's robe. They will find there, as nowhere else in the New World, a romantic blending of the past and present—the sixteenth and nineteenth centuries existing side by side "in harmonious discord." They will find that San Antonio is not so ultra-progressive as some of her sister cities—that her people have not yet cast aside humanity and anointed themselves with hypocrisy, like ancient runners with oil, for that race whose guerdon is gold. She does not give the stranger a stereotyped two-for-a-quarter smile, an ice-cream handshake, and expect to be repaid with a paean of praise that will send the price of real estate up 10 percent.

• • • • •

San Antonio possesses for the poet, the philosopher, and the student an inexpressible charm. Its skies are brighter than those of France, its airs softer than those of Italy. There Anglo-Saxon chivalry rose to its glorious zenith. There was fought America's Thermopylae. There Ben Milam led his Spartan band against the fortifications and five-fold force of General Cos, and fell, crowned with her victor's wreath. There was planted the standard of Christian faith when Texas was peopled by wild beasts and still more savage men. On the ancient battlements of San Antonio have floated the banners of six nations, and through her streets for a hundred and fifty years has ebbed and flowed the crimson tide of war.

Schools

To run a genius through a university were like running a young eagle through a threshing machine—it will require years for him to recover from his injuries.

• • • • •

Our educational system is Procrustean. It magnifies the mesquite but mangles the Cedars of Lebanon.

• • • • •

Lincoln is the only really great man America has yet produced—the only one who will be considered worth a hundred lines in the world's history a thousand years hence—and he was his own alma mater.

• • • • •

You can no more develop a Socrates by our public school system than you can hatch elephants in an incubator or breed a Bucephalus in a bird cage. Our public school system is simply a machine into which multifarious minds are thrown, as raw material, and transformed into so many mental shoe pegs. No attempt is made to measure the capabilities of the pupil—to determine whether Almighty God intended him for a poet or a pot walloper, a Massillon or a mule driver.

Separation of Church & State

That religion which must rely upon secular law is inherently rotten.

• • • • •

I believe in taxing luxuries, and a costly church is not a necessity. At least Christ didn't think so, for he never built one.

• • • • •

When all the pent-up antagonism to American Protestantism explodes, we may find the church declared a nuisance, and not only taxed, but compelled to pay a special license like the saloon and other supposed pests of the body social.

The South

In no section of this land of the alleged free and home of the ism does the blowhard blow longer and louder than in the South. We are the people, the nonpareil; there are none like us beneath the sun!

• • • • •

Women who desire to be beautiful cannot afford to remain in Michigan, where their complexions are exposed to the raw lake winds in winter and a broiling sun in summer. They must come South where balmy airs make the skin like velvet—airs so delicious that they involuntarily throw back their shoulders and inhale it until they resemble the high-breasted heroines of Homer.

• • • • •

The very moon and stars are brighter, and flood the earth with molten silver that transforms even a red barn into a fairy castle, a piebald mule into a Pegasus, and falling between softly sighing trees upon the dark grass gleams there like fathomless pools in which you expect to see the heavens reflected. The Spring is a sunburst of beauty, the glad earth green as an emerald and thick-sown with flowers, the woods fragrant Gardens of Gul, while along the crest of the hills, half hidden in purple haze, you catch in fancy fleeting glimpses of Diane's hamadryades, "with all their dewey hair blown back like flame"; the Autumn dreamy, delicious, subtle-sweet as music on a moonlit lake, along whose dark shore the fire flies sweep in lazy streams of flame amid flowers that fill the air with sensuous incense. If that doesn't fetch you, you may remain in Michigan.

• • • • •

During all the years I have resided South I have wondered why I didn't discover the superior advantages of this section sooner. Perhaps it was because I considered its chief products to be yellow fever and funerals, politicians and centipedes, cotton and Colonels, dysteleology and general damnation. I came South much as the average tourist visits Mexico—to see a strange country and a stranger people—but soon decided that 50 years of Dixie were better than a cycle of icicles.

South America

Had the famous Light Brigade charged the mobilized armies of South America it would not have lost a dozen men; but the chances are that every horse would have been stolen from under it.

The Southern Mercury

As the organ of Texas Populists the [*Southern*] *Mercury* could easily make a fortune if it had an editor, instead of an ignorant animal in its sanctum who thinks with his abdomen, writes with his feet, and employs his large porous ears for blotting pads. Physically he's a squab and mentally he's a resounding vacuum. When he thinks he's thinking with his brains he's only troubled with a rumbling of the bowels.

• • • • •

The Texas asylums being filled to overflowing, many harmless lunatics are allowed to run at large, but even with this advantage, if the *Southern Mercury* can prove 5,000 paid circulation, I'll do something desperate—I'll subscribe.

Saint Paul

It is said that his wife left him because he couldn't stop a calf without building a picket fence between his knees, and [was] so uncompromisingly homely that whenever he came near the family molasses, it fermented.

Sunday Laws

In every American state the people send a lot of yaps to the legislature—narrow-headed old stiffs and half-baked goslings—who imagine themselves duly commissioned to reform the human race and regulate the universe. The Gentleman from Somewhere introduces a bill making it a misdemeanor for a man to wiggle his toes or work his ears on the Sabbath day within seventeen miles of a deserted residence or twenty-nine miles of an empty church. The preachers gird on their armor and marshal the walleyed Sanctificationists and the free-love Holiness gang to the support of the measure. The business and professional men of the state make no protest, fear it might hurt their business to oppose the Meddlesome Matties. The bill becomes law—the state is shackled by a lot of canting old heifers in crummy underclothes, and hypocritical humbugs who peddle holiness for hire.

• • • • •

That extensive sect of sacred mummers declare it criminal to do on Sunday what is eminently proper on other days, and, being in a majority, they enact an ironclad law compelling Jew and Gentile to conform to their theological faith. And what excuse have they to offer for this insolent interference with individual liberty? [Reverend] Sam Jones sums it up when he says: "The people have no right to do wrong." True, oh Reverend Blatherskite, but who authorized you to decide for the American citizen who is right and wrong, theologically considered? Produce your credentials, Sir Garrulity, or come off the grass.

• • • • •

Good soul, who made thee thy brothers' keeper? Where in the constitution of your country or the teachings of your Saviour do you learn it to be your duty to lay violent hands upon a worldling and drag him, squirming and kicking—perhaps cursing—to the Throne of Grace? Produce your authority for employing the jails of this country to propagate the Christian religion—for cramming its forms and symbols down the throat of thy fellow man with a policeman's bludgeon. What is it to thee if I till my field, sell my goods, or listen to some aspiring Roscius spout Euripides on Sunday? Does it compel thee to do likewise? Does it interfere with your freedom or abridge your prerogatives, endanger your health or cost you a copper? Will the blessed Saviour compel you to answer for my sins and send you to hades as a "vicarious atonement" while I roost on some roseate cloud in company with a halo and a harp and attended by a choice assortment of she-angels! No? Then please to forbear further interference with my affairs. If I feel the need of your assistance to reach the Throne of Grace I'll so inform you.

• • • • •

We might at least expect that beneath the Lone Star, that especial child of liberty, the State would eschew the sacerdotal character and confine itself strictly to secular matters; yet her statutes make it a misdemeanor punishable by fine—which the offender must lay out in prison if he cannot pay—to labor, sell goods, or open a place of amusement in any section of the State, regardless of the religious predilections of the people.

• • • • •

It was a sultry summer afternoon in the City of Saints, called Waco by the common herd, but pronounced Wack-oh by those who have sold their cotton. Everybody who could borrow a dollar had excurted to other cities possessing less sanctification but more common sense, and the solemn stillness was broken only by the drowsy hum of a few perspiring pulpiteers who were making a feeble effort to earn their salaries by dealing damnation round on those who presumed to differ from their doxies. Not a leaf stirred, lest it be indicted for Sabbath desecration, the grass had stopped growing and the tawny Brazos quit running at twelve o'clock Saturday night, and the town cow gone outside the corporation to chew her cud. Everybody was full of ennui as a tariff editorial, slightly tempered by a faint hope of finding an excuse for committing a homicide. It was like being consigned alive to a secondhand sepulcher.

• • • • •

Ah me! Sunday's a dull day in Waco, for no one is permitted to do business but the hired preachers and the licensed prostitutes.

• • • • •

"But Sunday laws are necessary as a police regulation," I am told. Indeed? Is there aught in the Lord's day calculated to multiply criminal deeds? Is it possible that extra precautions must be taken on Emperor Constantine's "Holy Sabbath" to stay the hand of the homicide? Can it be that when a million Christian prayers are ascending like incense to the Throne of God—and ten thousand preachers turning an honest penny—that people are seized with an unnatural impulse to despoil their neighbors? This being the conceded effect of the Christian Sabbath it would appear desirable to abolish it altogether "as a police regulation" and the sooner the better.

T

Reverend Talmage's Dream of Heaven

My old friend, Rev. T. DeWitt Talmage, has been having another vision of heaven. DeWitt has an unfortunate habit of filling his pod with pickled pigs' feet and cold mince pie, sleeping on his back while his mouth gives an imitation of the Hoosac Tunnel. This is about the forty-'leventh time DeWitt has imagined himself pottering about the golden streets of the Sacred City. I was editing a daily paper when he was afflicted with one of those syndicate "dreams," and by some mistake we got the foolish thing in type three days before it was supposed to have occurred. If he really does dream such ridiculous things he should either change his diet or come to Texas and ride wild mustangs and raise 6-cent cotton until he can digest a raw dog. It is a duty he owes to the Christian faith to ring himself down, for no sane man wants to go to the heaven he assumes to see. You couldn't give me a title to the entire place conditioned that I remove thither from Texas. I'd soon pull off one of the pearly gates and sling it at one of the perpetual serenaders. I don't mind a little melody run in between lemonades; but I'm taking no stock in a German band wound up to last an eternity without pausing for beer or breath. A man who dreams of heaven as Talmage pretends he does (but doesn't) is a stupid savage whose highest concept of happiness is a perpetual circus. In all his stertorous pilgrimages to heaven he has never discovered the inhabitants doing aught in which a man of sense could take the slightest interest. They appear to be always glorifying—throwing bouquets at Father, Son, and Holy Ghost. I cannot imagine the Trinity finding satisfaction in the eternal soft soap of a gang of triflers who escaped hell only by the skin of their teeth. Think of the Creator of the Cosmos being tickled throughout all eternity by the cringing adulation of a Talmage, by millions of slaves ever circling 'round his throne and crying "Holy! Holy! Holy!"—wriggling on their bellies like a tubful of angleworms after a summer shower and charivariing him with cymbals, harps, and horns! I don't believe that he permits any such pachalic poppycock in Paradise. Perhaps Bro. Talmage could be happy in such a heaven; but I—I'd raise hell.

Teachers

We are making too many teachers of second-growth timber.

• • • • •

I have seen men at the head of public instruction in great States who spelled water with two t's, and superintendents of city schools who could not explain the difference between an excise and an import tax. Promotion of teachers, like kissing, goes by favor, and men officiate as members of schoolboards who cannot name the States of the American Union.

Texas

These balmy days, I often recall my ideas of Texas before I had the pleasure of mingling with its people—of becoming myself a Texan. After living in Texas for ten years I paid a visit to my people beyond the beautiful Ohio. The old gentlemen sized me up critically, evidently expecting to see me wearing war paint and a brace of Bowie knives. "So, young man, You're living in Texas?" "Yes, Paw." "Fell kinder to 'hum 'mong them centerpedes, cowboys 'n other varments, I s'pose?" "Y-y-yes, Paw." "Well, Billy, you allers was a mighty bad boy. I kinder cackalated as how you'd go t'hell some day; but, praise God, I never thought y' was bound for Texas!"

• • • • •

Texas can furnish forth more hidebound dogmatists, narrow-brained bigots, and intolerant fanatics in proportion to population than can any other section of these United States. That is why *The Iconoclast* located in Texas.

O dammit!

• • • • •

The Iconoclast receives a great many letters from people in distant states making inquiries about Texas in general and Waco in particular. The impression seems to be general among our trans-Ohio cousins that the Geyser City is simply a trading station on the borders of civilization where the "Apostle" has located for the conversion of the Indians—that the principal products of the state are cacti and general cussedness, cowboys and postbellum colonels.

• • • • •

I will say to those who have applied to *The Iconoclast* for information that they might do much worse than come to Texas. They can find here any kind of climate and soil they care to call for. Alpine claims to have had a snowstorm in July, and the musical hum of the mosquito ushers in the glad new year at Galveston, and rises, like a paean of praise, at Brownsville on Washington's birthday. While the norther in the Panhandle is taking an inventory of every bone in the human body, the Bohemian Club at Houston will be dallying in the shade of magnolia trees and conning its catechism. The soil in some sections is best adapted to the production of mesquite beans and mule-eared rabbits, while in others it is so prolific that an old corset plowed under will develop into a New Woman, and a pair of discarded suspenders if properly planted and "hilled" will produce a candidate for Congress. If he is looking for an urban location he will find Waco a progressive little city, situated on the tawny Brazos at the head of navigation. Its chief institutions are *The Iconoclast* and Baylor University. One can readily see that a city possessing such a combination of purity and genius is bound to progress. The man who has money which is burning in his pockets will find here ample opportunity for its investment. We may be far out on the fringe of civilization, but I trust we realize that the gentle stranger, who comes to us in his guileless faith, should be taken in.

• • • • •

Taffy does not grow on trees in Texas.

• • • • •

No Alps or Apennines burst from Texas's broad bosom and rear their cold, dead peaks mile above mile into heaven's mighty vault; no Vesuvius belches his lurid, angry flame at the stars like a colossal cannon worked by Titans at war with the Heavenly Hierarchy; no Niagara churns its green waters into rainbow-tinted foam. The grandeur of Texas is not that of destruction and desolation; its beauties are not those which thrill the heart with awe, but fill it with adoration and sweet content. Not dark and dreary mountains riven by the bolts of angry Jove; not gloomy Walpurgis gorges where devils dance and witches shriek; not the savage thunder of the avalanche, but the sun-kissed Valley of Cashmere, the purple hills of the lotus eaters' land, the pastoral beauties of Tempe's delightful vale.

• • • • •

The fates are turning upon Texas an unkindly eye. A lone highwayman has held up and robbed a populous passenger train in Texas—in West Texas, the rendezvous of the sure-enough bad man, who catches catamounts and clips their claws, who defies whole barrels o' Jersey lightning and uses the bucking bronco for his laughter, yea, his sport! Shades o' Ben Thompson and Luke Short, has it come to this—that a rank stranger can lasso a Texas train, drive the passengers under the seats, plunder them at his pleasure, with no one to molest or make him afraid! Half a hundred Texans trembling at the sight of one gun were a sight worth seeing—and they did not even know it was loaded! . . . Alas, poor Texas!

A Texas Norther Explained on a Hot Summer Day

A gentleman at Sioux City, Iowa, appeals to *The Iconoclast* to inform him "what a Texas norther may be." A Texas norther, my Christian friend, may be, and usually is, very much of a nuisance. It is much like a spring day in Iowa—a cold, dank, windy, watery wetness. A norther is a Dakota blizzard that has gotten off the reservation and lost its bearings. It usually comes down on Sioux City first like a wolf on the fold, then makes a Fitzsimmons swipe at Omaha. Then it drops a tear on the pine tombstone of the erstwhile Jesse James and blows into the mouth of the Kaw just to see if it's loaded. It then starts across Kansas, but usually becomes frightened by the female reformers, and it comes a-chortling down into the Indian Territory and makes Lo the poor Indian yearn for a five-finger snifter of bootleg booze and a new government blanket. If it doesn't break its mainspring crossing Red River, it introduces itself to the people of Denison as a full-fledged Texas norther. The norther is bad enough in all conscience, but is to the blizzard what varioloid is to confluent smallpox, or lager beer to Prohibition booze. It is the thin edge of a northern winter which inserts itself into this earthly Eden semi-occasionally, much to our dissatisfaction. It usually catches a man seven miles from home without his overcoat. Sometimes it wanders as far south as Waco and evokes audible wishes that the Yankee[s] would keep their d——d weather for their consumption. About the time you get a stove up and trusted for a ton of coal, the norther is dead as Hector, the hokeypokey man is again on the warpath, the kids are rolling on the grass in the glad sunshine, and the gude housewife is chasing a marauding hen out of the flower garden. That, my dear sir, is all I know about northers. If you can deliver an able-bodied one at this office during the next ten days you will hear of something to your advantage.

Texas Politics

Take the unsavory stew of MacBeth's witches, season with ipecac, perfume with asafetida, and you get an *olla podrida* resembling Texas politics. We have Populists filled with pop and Prohibitionists full of prunes; we have two brands of Republicans, Mugwumps of every degree, and all kinds and conditions of Democrats. I am trying to perfect an apparatus that will enable me to photograph this Proteus of politics. It is the only animal on earth that goes forwards, backwards, and progresses to the right while it is moving to the left. It can turn inside out, swallow its own corporosity, sit down upon itself, and talk at the same time.

The Traveling Salesman

The "Drummer" is distinctly an American institution. If we did not invent, we developed him. He is not unknown to other lands, but the practice of "drumming trade" has been brought to the highest perfection in this hustling, pushing Republic of the West. The day has gone by when it were possible to build up a profitable business without hard and persistent hustling—and that's what the Drummer is here for. But he is more than an important trade factor; he is an apostle of civilization, nay, of religion itself—the religion of humanity. He penetrates every city, town, and hamlet, bringing the people of the various sections of our common country into closer fellowship, making stupid provincialism impossible. He has wiped out Mason and Dixon's line. He is a public educator, a disseminator of new ideas, an inculcator of tolerance for the opinion of others. He carries into the country the polish of the city, into the city the vigor of the country. With all due respect to the "cloth," I believe we could better spare the D.D.s for a thousand years than the Drummers for one day.

Truth

Truth and only Truth is eternal. It was not born and it cannot die. It may be obscured by the clouds of falsehood, or buried in the debris of brutish ignorance, but it can never be destroyed. It exists in every atom, lives in every flower, and flames in every star. When the heavens and the earth shall pass away and the universe return to cosmic dust, divine truth will stand unscathed amid the crash of matter and the wreck of worlds.

• • • • •

A thing may be true though all the world dispute it, or false if everyone believe it.

U

The Universe

Of course it is as easy to conceive of matter without a Creator as to conceive of a Creative Power without an origin. It is perfectly legitimate to ask, "If God made the universe, who made God?" To that I can only answer that I do not know—that the finite mind cannot grasp infinity, that the query is entirely too large for my intellect; but while the birth of a god is even a greater miracle than uncreated matter, when we see that matter governed by immutable laws we may reasonably infer a lawgiver.

W

Waco

Although its natural advantages are superior to those of any other Texas city, it is the sixth in size. That's because it imagines that it can work industrial wonders by drinking toasts and feeding its face. At the businessmen's banquet given a few nights ago, and at which enough new enterprises were outlined to appall Chicago, were enthusiastic whoopers-up who haven't paid their grocery bills in three months. Yet they got full o' champagne punch and prunes and told what we, us & co., are going to do to make Waco great. But the wonderful schemes of commercial grandeur faded next morning with the champagne fumes. Waco gets rid of entirely too much nervo-muscular energy in unprofitable gab. She does an infinite deal of cackling but lays no eggs. She is the past grand architect of castles in Spain. Her intentions are all right, but her execution has a broken mainspring. She is constant to one thing never, but starves between divers dazzling schemes.

• • • • •

Waco is a maelstrom, not of religion, but of religiosity. Her eyes are ever in "a fine frenzy rolling." She is filled with faith, but can give no valid reason therefore. She is not God-intoxicated, but drunk with the odor of her own Pseudo-sanctity and oblivious to the sweet reasonableness of things, deaf to whatsoever doesn't begin with an alleluiah and end with an awmen. She's going it blind, no blessed lamp of Logic, no moral balance—trying to lift herself to Jesus by pulling desperately by her own emotional umbilicus.

O dammit!

• • • • •

Waco is forever making a large piebald ass of herself. She is always ready to promise to put up a dollar and six bits for a penny whistle but wouldn't obligate herself to give, on the installment plan, seven and a quarter for a grand piano with all modern improvements. Were the majestic universe for sale for $10 cash, she'd fail to make connections—would get hopelessly sidetracked while conferring, banqueting, whereasing, resoluting, perorating, and otherwise agitating the atmosphere.

• • • • •

Waco is the religious storm centre of the universe, and one of the few places that licenses prostitution—a fact for the consideration of students of cause and effect.

• • • • •

I can take $50,000 and make Jack the Ripper mayor of Waco; but the Lord Jesus Christ could not be elected strictly on his merits.

• • • • •

For the information of the effete East, *The Iconoclast* will state that while the present population of Waco is a trifle less than of London, the city has greater room in which to grow; and as her people are chiefly of the Baptist breed, the natural increase must ere long place her at the head of the procession. Waco is indeed a land flowing with milk and honey. Her streets are so smooth that a mountain goat can traverse them with comparative ease, and so clean that it is seldom that a mule gets lost in the mud. The tax rate is so low that if your property be well located you can usually persuade the collector to accept it as partial payment. Of course, Waco, like other places, has its drawbacks; but taken by and large, there is no better. While it is true that you cannot secure a bath, shave, or clean shirt here on Sunday, the saloons and churches are open. Waco's good people are not quite all in the cemetery. It boasts two or three society women who do not chew gum, straddle a bike, nor drink gin rickeys. There are several men here who could safely be left alone with a blind orphan girl, or a corpse whose eyes were covered with coppers.

• • • • •

There are many Waco merchants from whom I would accept change for a dollar without counting it to see if it was correct, or expecting to find the dimes all Mexican and the nickels all plugged. There are two or three preachers in town to whom I would listen with respect if I had nothing better to do. On the whole, Waco is not such a bad place after all, and may escape destruction, if, like Lot, I wrestle for it valiantly with the Lord.

• • • • •

"If you don't like Waco, why don't you pack up your traps and leave?"—Indignant Citizen.

Peccavi! By which "Indig. Cit." will please understand that I have sinned and am sorry.

Epilogue

In the last months of The Iconoclast, *William Brann became weary of his little paper "and the infernal wrangling" it produced. Distressed by the firestorm of violence caused by his attacks on Baylor and Waco's Baptists, he began using outside material from "correspondents" and repeated essays from earlier editions. He started a novel and a play. What he wrote for* The Iconoclast *was more introspective, philosophic, as though he needed to explain himself, his beliefs, to those who attacked him.*

The Iconoclast Speaks

I shall not quarrel with a world I do not understand.

• • • • •

I realize that there has been no era without its burden of sorrow, no time without its fathomless lake of tears; that the past seems more glorious than the present because the heart casts a glamour over days that are dead. From the dust and glare of the noon of life we cast regretful glances back to the dewy morn, and as the eye creeps on, the shadows reach further back until they link the cradle and the grave and all is dark.

• • • • •

The Sacred Books of all the centuries are essentially the same—the half articulate voice of the world crying for light, the frantic efforts of man to learn whence he came and whither he goes, to lift the veil that shrouds the two eternities—to see and know! I gather them together—the Old Testament and the New, the Koran and the sacred Vedas, the northern Sagas and the southern Mythologies; I search them through, not to scoff, but to gather, with reverent soul, every gleam of light that since the birth of Time has been vouchsafed to man. I read the Revelations and ponder the Prophecies; I listen once again to the voice of Memnon answer to the rosy fingers of the morn. I sit with Siddartha beneath the Bodhi tree and follow the prophet of Islam in all his pilgrimages; I stand with Moses on Sinai's flaming crest and listen to the prayer of Christ in the Garden of Gethsemane, then I go forth beneath the eternal stars—each silent, pouring its stream of sidereal fire into the great realm of Darkness—and they seem like the eyes of pitying angels, watching man work out, little by little, through the long ages, the mystery of life.

• • • • •

We know not whence we came or what for, whither we go or what we'll do when we get there. True it is that life is not altogether labor and lees—there's some skittles and beer; but the most of us get more shadow than sunshine. . . . Man born of woman is of few days and full of politics. The moment he hits the globe he starts for the grave, and his only visible reward for long days of labor and nights of pain is an epitaph he can't read and a tombstone he don't want.

• • • • •

Not to the past, but to the future, do I look for the Saturnian age, when the demons of need and greed will be exorcised, when love will be the universal law, the fatherhood of God the only faith. Such, my friends, is the rainbow to which I have turned my feet. It lies afar, across dismal swamps o'er whose icy summits only the condor's shadow sweeps—across arctic vast and desert isles beyond tempestuous ocean rank with dead men's bones and the rotting hulls of ships. I shall not attain it, nor shall you, but he that strives, though vanquished, still is victor. A dreamer, say you? Ah yes, but all life is but a dream, mystic, wonderful, and we know not when we sleep nor when we wake. I love to dream so when the storm beats upon the great oaks, hoary with their hundred years, and they put forth their gnarled arms and grapple with the blast; when the lightning cleaves the inky sky with forked flame and the earth rocks 'neath the thunder's angry roar; when the dark clouds roll muttering unto the East and the evening sun hangs every leaf and twig and blade of grass with jewels brighter than e'er gleamed in Golconda's mines; when the mock-birds renew their melody and every flower seems drunken with its own incense, I look upon the irisate glory that seems to belt the world with beauty and my heart beats high with hope that in years to be the storm clouds that o'ershadow the souls of men will recede also—that time will come when the human race will be one universal brotherhood. . . .

• • • • •

For ten years the Protestant clergy have waged unrelenting warfare upon me for presuming to exercise the American prerogative of free speech—for disagreeing with them [they] have denounced me with more vigor than they brought to bear on the Devil. They have demanded my discharge from editorial positions and advocated boycotts on newsdealers who handled papers on which I was employed. Yet I never spoke disparagingly of their religion or denied their Deity.

• • • • •

I was taught that this was a land of liberty, where every man is privileged to worship God in his own way, or ignore him altogether; that it was my duty to insist upon this right, both for myself and for my fellows.

• • • • •

I once entertained the idea that so long as I spoke reverently of God and respectfully of all religions, I would expose hypocrites and humbugs without offending the average run of church people, but I know better now.

• • • • •

. . . [N]ot one of them ever tried to convert me. Not one of them ever tried, by kindly argument, to convince me that I was wrong. Not one of them ever invited me to church—or prayed for me, so far as I could learn. Perhaps they thought I was past redemption.

• • • • •

I could never make a success in the role of other-cheek Christian.

• • • • •

My position as court of last resort for the Baptists of this country is no sinecure. The brethern and sisters frequently quarrel among themselves, then appeal to me to "roast" or even excommunicate each other. Sometimes they even indulge in free fights, burn churches, or commit sinful acts that make my heart bleed and cause me to fear that I will never be able to recommend them to Saint Peter for admission into Paradise. I've labored and wept and prayed with them until my patience is worn to a frazzle, but the more intense their religious zeal the more frequent their rows. Sometime they turn and lick the umpire. . . .

• • • • •

We are solemnly assured that the world is steadily growing better, and I suppose that's so, for in days of old they crucified men head downwards for telling the truth, while now they only hammer them over the head with six-shooters and drag 'em around a Baptist campus with a rope. All that a reformer now needs is a hard head and a rubber neck.

• • • • •

If Socrates was poisoned and Christ was crucified for telling unpalatable truths to the splenetic-hearted hypocrites of their time, it would ill become me to complain of a milder martyrdom for a like offense.

• • • • •

To the kindly offers of other cities to afford *The Iconoclast* an asylum and protect its editor from outrage, I will simply say that I do not consider either my property or person in the slightest danger. A majority of the Texas people are both broad-guaged and law-abiding. We probably have our proportion of intolerant bigots and splentic-hearted little blatherskites who preach mob violence from the pulpit; but such people are not dangerous so long as they are well watched. My forbears helped make Texas a republic; they helped make it a state of the American union. I like the climate, and most of the people, and am in no hurry to move. I may have to seek a better distributing point for my publications, as they are already too extensive to be properly handled from any Texas town, but I shall not pull my tent stakes for a day or two. If I do move—sometime within the next twelve months—it will be bruited throughout the universe that I was driven out of Waco; but that won't worry my soul a cent's worth. I've been lied about so d____n much that I feel ill at ease and neglected unless the target of vindictive mendacity by tearful souls who fail to pay their debts. I've been kept so badly frightened all month [November, 1897] by threats to drag me out of my home and hang me, or otherwise measure me up for a crop of angelic pinfeathers that I've been unable to write anything worth reading. But as soon as I can swallow my heart and quit shivering, I will grab the English language by the butt-end and make it crack like a new bullwhip about the ears and humbugs. Meanwhile I desire to state that there is nothing the matter with *The Iconoclast*'s contributors. They are a bouquet of pansy blossoms of whom any publisher might well be proud. Should the editor chance to swallow too much water the next time he is baptized, they can be depended upon to keep the flag of *The Iconoclast* afloat until the red-headed heir-apparent learns to write with one hand and shoot with the other. Let it go at that.

• • • • •

I walk the streets of Waco day by day, and I walk them alone. Let these cur-ristians shoot me in the back if they dare. . . . If the decent people of this community fail to chase them to their holes and feed their viscera to the dogs, then I'd rather be dead and in hades forever then alive in Waco a single day.

The Final Word

Long after William Brann's burial in Waco's Oakwood Cemetery, friends erected a monument to his memory. The gravestone contains a bas-relief *profile of the iconoclast. Someone fired two shots at the stone, one bullet striking the profile in the temple. The scars are visible today. The marker has only Brann's initials and the raised profile. No identifying mark at all, just a single word: Truth.*

O dammit!

An Evening with The Iconoclast

A play in two parts
by Jerry Flemmons

Set

The stage is furnished sparsely, suggesting rather than re-creating a magazine office of the 1890s. The office is in a central downtown Waco, Texas, building. Outside are Franklin Street and Fourth Street. If a window existed, William Brann could see the Pacific Hotel with its adjacent bar commonly called George Laneri's Saloon, French's Newsstand, and the entrance to Banker's Alley, a narrow walkway beside the hotel.

Office furnishings are a period rolltop desk and worn padded chair. The desk's top is open and the audience can see the paper clutter of a writer and editor. Beside the desk is a coatrack. Nearby are a tall pigeonhole flattop table and high stool. The table is cluttered. A wastebasket overflows with discarded papers.

The time is April 1, 1898.

The curtain always is up.

In the absence of a proper or adequate stage, *O dammit!* may be performed with an antique lectern and small table on which to place various necessary papers.

Playwright's Note

Pre-curtain ragtime music seems to convey best the mood of Brann's era.

Using descriptions by his biographer, Charles Carver, period photographs, and self-revelatory gleanings from his writings, it is possible to reconstruct William Brann's physical appearance and lectern style at one of those stage appearances by the iconoclast.

He is tall, almost Lincolnesque in stature, and has a hard, lean strength to his body which he carries straight, unbent, as a kind of dignified protective tower for his more unsanctified ideas and thoughts. His near-gauntness is exaggerated by large expressive hands. The hands of Brann, and his clear baritone voice, are the instruments of his iconoclastic style and he has a virtuosic control of each. The hands can be, as he chooses, battering rams against the hypocrisy of his age, or gentle sculpturing tools for the creation of eloquent flights of imagination. Often, one hand grasps a large cigar for use as an effective symbolic rapier or, as a stage device, a prop for dramatic emphasis. The accentless voice can be Shakespearean grandiloquence or Texas twang, insolent or conciliatory, aristocratic or folksy, sharp or soft, menacing or congenial, arrogant or self-deprecating, self-assured or doubting, mannered or crude. Above all else, he is a natural actor, a preacher and a teacher with a message, and to serve his viewpoints he uses all that he has at his command.

On stage, Brann is an imposing figure who, above all else, enjoys himself. He dresses in a formal black suit styled in the 1890s manner, a vest holding a pocket watch and gold chain, suspenders, white shirt, and black bow tie sagging at the ends. His jacket sleeves are slightly short, emphasizing his large hands. Brann's hair is dark, full over the ears and at the back, side-parted, mildly pompadoured. He has a straight Roman nose, firm chin, and ebony eyes under black brows. He is clean-shaven.

On April 1, 1898, the day of his death, Brann is forty-three, and he is energized, ebullient, because he is leaving the next day on a lengthy lecture tour which promises to be both intellectually and financially profitable, and an escape from the stress of six months' violence in Waco.

In many instances, I have retained *The Iconoclast*'s eccentric style of writing: the emphasized capitalization, the comma-crammed punctuation, the archaic words such as anent and yawp, the euphemistic spelling, e.g., damphool for "damn fool." I've even preserved the strange adjective, Squeeritic, simply because it sounds right in context. I can find nothing about Squeeritic in the usual reference books and have no intention of chasing the word to its source for fear I will discover it is misused.

Antonia Teixeira's last name is pronounced: Tay-Hay-Rah.

Brann's middle name, Cowper, is pronounced: Coo-per. Doubtless, he was named for the English poet, William Cowper.

Prologue

(Actor enters as himself. He is dressed in costume but without coat and jacket. The jacket hangs on the coatrack. The vest is on the chair back. He moves downstage, speaks to audience.)

A long time ago, more than a century now, William Brann was a famous writer and lecturer. Lecturer . . . writer . . . editor . . . publisher: he was the entire staff of *The Iconoclast,* a magazine read by almost a million people every month all across America and around the world.

He called it a magazine, though from all appearances it was little more than a pamphlet. It didn't look like much. There were no illustrations, no covers, nothing to mark it as extraordinary or important . . . except the writing and style, and its universal message of humanity.

(Actor puts on vest as he speaks)

William Brann would have worked in an office such as this, a cluttered office overflowing with the debris of a man whose inventory was words and ideas. He was unafraid of ideas, certainly he was unafraid of expressing ideas, the substance of which often angered and disturbed readers . . . but never bored them. He wrote at a desk like this, hunched over, scribbling on long pads in his passionate, searing prose style. And he would have lectured to an audience such as you, intimately, in a folksy way, yet theatrically and grandly. This is his office, this is his stage, and we are in the past of long ago.

Outside is Waco, downtown Waco, a pleasant, small town in the 1890s of Central Texas. It was a nice place to live but a curious hamlet from which to publish America's most controversial magazine, one whose contents made its neighbors uncomfortable and often angry.

And it is a Friday in spring. April first. The Bluebonnets have come to the fields, and purple verbena, and there are new yellow buttercups along the creek banks. The trees have budded with what poet Robert Burns once called "little mouse ear leaves." The year is 1898, a long ago time of an era we now remember as calmer and more serene.

(He finds old newspaper on desk, scans as though reading)

Let's see . . . the news of 1898 . . . President and Mrs. McKinley, it says here, will summer at a hotel near Lake Champlain. We are at war again, this time against Spain over Cuba. A young colonel named Roosevelt . . . Teddy . . . has recruited a troop of horse soldiers, mostly from Texas. The recession, that one which began back in '93, has about run its course, but inflation is still raging. Why, potatoes have gone to twenty-five cents a peck! And boned ham is ten cents a pound! Galvanized washtubs, fifty-three cents each. Men's summer tan shoes, $3.95 the pair, just reduced. Here is local news: "The Widow Anderson's cow died of indigestion and strangulation on Wednesday. She was a good milker and the main support of her owner."

(Folds paper on desk, moves to coatrack)

A tragedy for Mrs. Anderson. Tragedy is magnified in small towns. William Brann understood that.

(Puts on jacket, checks pocket watch for time)

He knew about us, about people, how we laughed and loved and cried. He was a man of large passions who understood that what he thought and said often distressed others.

William Brann once wrote of his reluctance to give advice. He said: "There is peril in it. Remember the lesson of Socrates. He went around Old Athens giving advice to people. . . . They poisoned him."

(Exits)

Act One

(Brann enters with a packet of mail and newspapers. He selects a newspaper that interests him, and drops the remainder amid the desk clutter. He scans the newspaper and moves downstage. In a bemused manner, he says:)

There is, according to this, today's edition of the *Waco Weekly Tribune,* two men on Earth who are doomed to be damned . . . that Great Atheist, Robert Ingersoll, and myself! The damner is a local preacher who has announced to his congregation that he will no longer pray for us.

Well . . . that do settle it!

For how can we hope to make a celestial landing without his help? This almighty man having declined to exercise his pull with the Heavenly powers in our behalf, we get no corner lot in the New Jerusalem, not even a perch among the feathered Angels. This Waco sky-pilot is going to slip his hawser and sail for the Heavenly henceforth, leaving we two behind. If we stretch forth our arms he will not heed us. If we lift up our voices in sad lament, the cruel answer will come floating back from the fast-receding Ship of Zion:

"Lost! Lost! Lost . . . Forever!"

. . . in Waco, Texas.

Welcome to Waco!

. . . home of we Dissipated, Dispossessed souls. Cynosure of the known Universe, and all parts South.

Sixth largest city in this grand state! The Athens of Texas, as some will have you believe, because of our four famed religious educational institutions. Or, as the rowdy crowd names it: Six-Shooter Depot! Because it is as easy to be shot here as receive a Baptist education.

Either may be fatal.

Population on this fine Spring day of 1898: thirty thousand. Though not a man can tell you how many are here temporarily to test the curative powers of Waco's renowned mineral water geysers. Waco is becoming a famous watering-hole. She has, after all, the finest bathhouse in the world . . . a Baptist University. Between our battalions of total-submersion baptizing Baptists and the geyser doctors, Waco dunks almost everyone who crosses the city line.

(Shuffles through desk clutter to find pamphlet)

As local pamphleteers assert, our miraculous waters can rid you of . . .

(Reads)

". . . chronic rheumatism, gout, eczema, neuralgia, blood poisoning . . . Syphilis in All Forms . . . epilepsy, hysteria, alcoholism, Saint Vitus Dance, nervous prostration, and insomnia."

In connection with the latter affliction, a Mr. Luther Tinsley of Fort Worth testifies by witnessed deposition that "because of her restlessness and nervousness, I had been unable to sleep with my wife for ten years. After only two treatments of your mineral water . . . anybody can sleep with her!"

In short, Waco can cure you of just about anything, except religious ecstasy and homesickness.

Waco, I would have you know, is the religious storm centre of the Universe, and one of the few places that licenses prostitution . . . a fact for consideration of students of cause and effect. She is well-supplied with a saloon in every block, a church 'round every corner, and a fire or a failure every day. Being deeply religious, Waco takes her motto from the Bible: "He that provideth not for his own household is worse than an infidel." Which means: though we may be far out on the fringe of civilization, we realize that the gentle stranger, who comes to us in his guileless faith . . . should be taken in.

Welcome to Waco!

(In more serious, folksy tone)

Ladies and Gentlemen, I am William Cowper Brann, publisher and editor of *The Iconoclast.* There are many things which I cordially dislike, but my pet aversion is the set lecture . . . one of those stereotyped affairs ground out with studied inflection and practiced gesture. Hence I shall ask permission to speak informally and freely as though we were seated around the soda fount of a Windy City drug store.

I want you to feel open to disagree as if we had gotten into this difficulty by accident instead of design. It is not required that we agree on everything, for if we did, it would be obvious one of us is unnecessary.

(Checks time with pocket watch)

I see we are off to a prompt start. Before we begin in earnest . . . are there any gentlemen of the press with us?

(Looks into audience, generally in front rows, and counts)

One, two? Four . . . seven? So many? Have all the saloons run dry at once? Good! I was afraid my reputation had gone to the bow-wows. Gentlemen, ask me all the questions you want to. I confess that I am a veritable reservoir of knowledge, an encyclopedic basin . . . that I know, in truth, absolutely nothing, and that not well. I, as a quarrelsome critic once wrote of me, am often wrong, but always certain, that I have nothing to say, but say it so entertainingly that audiences long to hear me say it again. I am no orator as Brutus but simply a plain, blunt man, like Marc Antony, who spoke right on and said what he did know, or thought he knew, which was just as satisfactory to himself. He's dead now, poor fellow. Woman in the case, of course.

The Iconoclast, I am pleased to admit, is the only American magazine ever to have secured a quarter of a million monthly readership. A dollar per annum by subscription, ten cents each number. It is an independent American journal, exercising its constitutional prerogative to say what seemeth unto it best, without asking any man's permission. *The Iconoclast* does not expect that it will reform the world, will drag in the Golden Age by the ears, or pull the millennium before it is ripe. If it does exceed in exposing a few Frauds and peeling the cuticle from an occasional Fake, it will not have lived and died in vain.

(Listens to reporter)

An Iconoclast? Sir, for a journalist, your etymological ignorance is intolerable. I refer you to an author who doubtless is a stranger: Mr. Webster.

(Opens dictionary on desk, thumbs to correct page)

He explains Iconoclast as "one who attacks cherished beliefs and traditional institutions as being based on error or superstition."

From the Greek *I-con,* meaning "Idol," and *klas-tes,* meaning "Breaker." Thus, a "breaker of idols." I confine my weapons to words because, as the Waco Baptists have proved to me, this is not a safe and sure occupation. My back is sore still from the last sermon they administered.

(Listens to reporter)

Why am I an Iconoclast?

(Thoughtful pause)

Why not?

This world has enough perfidious villains. We need optimism. Why not my impudent brand of fearless hope? The optimist is a good gift in life. He is the brass band in the political procession, the Hallelujah at a Methodist camp meeting. Overtaken by a deluge, we optimists do not drown, but like champagne corks, bob serenely to the surface.

I am an Iconoclast because man has a tendency to become what he believes himself to be, and because the more a man knows, the more he doubts. Too many men make their minds cold-storage warehouses for other people's ideas, because the average human head, like an egg or a crock of clabber, absorbs the flavor of its surroundings. Far too many men much resemble Mark Twain's frog with its stomach full of buckshot. They are crushed to Earth by the things they have swallowed.

In my life I have believed many things with all my soul only to find them false. Our ideas change. The wisest men in the world once believed this Earth was flat. They believed in witches, thought the sky a canvas tent, and the stars holes for the rain to pour through.

O dammit!

And those were the intellectuals!

Sir, I am a seeker of Truth. Life has a limited circulation and no assurance of a second edition, thus I want my answers now. My philosophy is: when you get an idea, put it on the anvil and bid the world hit it with the heaviest sledge. The more you hammer Truth the brighter it becomes. That's what my little paper is for.

Are my Truths real? The insanity expert believes everyone crazy but himself.

Why here? This is fertile ground, my friend. Texas can furnish forth more hidebound dogmatists, narrow-minded bigots and intolerable fanatics in proportion to population than can any other section of these United States!

Welcome to Waco!

The Iconoclast is read in all America, and in foreign nations, and in sub-exotic locales such as Houston. There, in the Year of our Lord, 1891, I was pole-axed by an idea for a new kind of publication. Being at the time Chief Editorial Writer on the *Houston Post*, I felt dreadfully mortified, as no real idea had ever before occurred in that morally impotent establishment. Thus disqualified for work at the *Post*, I took sanctuary in the village of Austin, where I began *The Iconoclast*, which eventually, and naturally, gravitated to Waco, the political and religious ganglion of the state.

Immediately, *The Iconoclast* prospered and, toiling in this dogmatic kennel as missionary to the Presbyterians and Campbellites, Baptists and Methodists, and other minor religious brotherhoods, I became an evangelist of great fame. I became . . .

(With assumed pomposity)

. . . The Apostle!

I did not invent this salubrious subtitle, but had it thrust upon me by the Reverend T. DeWitt Talmage of Washington, D.C., that celebrated preacher who parts his hair in the middle and his name on the side. Though I believe Brother Talmage meant: Apostle . . . of the Devil!

Fair enough. I confess a sneaking respect for Satan, for he is preeminently a success in his chosen profession. He sat in on the game with cash capital of one snake. Now he's got half the world grabbed and an option on the other half.

Perhaps Brother Talmage knows something I do not. After all, he attracts the largest audience of any American preacher.

(Searches on table for paper)

Herein is his latest urgent message, titled "Bricks Without Straw." I'll spare you the reading of it but my critique is that it is a rambling fragmentary piece of mental hodgepodge, in which scraps of school book Egyptology, garbled Bible stories, false political economy, and fragments of misapplied history tumble over each other like specters in a delirium.

Last week the *Tyler Telegram* humbly apologized for calling this wide-lipped blatherskite a "Religious fakir." Next thing you know our Tyler contemporary will apologize for having Inadvertently hazarded the statement that water is wet. When a daily newspaper tells the truth . . . even by accident . . . it should stick with it. The man who can find intellectual food in Talmage's sermons could acquire a case of delirium tremens by drinking the froth out of a pop bottle.

(Softer, folksy)

In truth, I thank God every day for having created Talmage. From an anthropological standpoint, he is the Greatest Show on Earth, and is, to my riper years, what Old Dan Rice's single-ring circus was to my youth.

My Alpha years, though, were entertained by few circuses. I first saw light in Coles County, Illinois. My mother died when I was two. My father, a country Presbyterian minister of no earthly possessions except me and my sister, gave us to a farmer, William Hawkins.

Farmer Hawkins was a God-fearing man whom God as well would have feared had he lived in Mr. Hawkins's house. He believed in hard work for boys. I did not.

I became an apprentice sinner, and prospered at the craft.

At age thirteen, I left to become an itinerant, and have done pretty much everything a man may do and dodge the penitentiary, except run for office and make Fourth of July speeches: hotel bellboy, grainer, printer's devil, railroad brakeman. I pitched on a semiprofessional baseball team, even managed a touring opera company.

O dammit!

By hard work and careful attention to detail . . . I failed at all.

And being at twenty-one, a life-long, habitual failure, I deemed myself sufficiently prepared for marriage. I took for my wife Miss Carrie Belle Martin. My beloved Carrie had lifted me from failure. Soon afterwards, our first child, Inez, was born.

(Pause, softer)

My dear . . . dear Inez.

(Pause)

Marriage hurled me into responsibility and I took my first job as a writer on the *St. Louis Globe-Dispatch.* I was in the game to stay. Later, I came to Texas, to invent this Great Religious Monthly of mine, with which I finally have found success. I don't wish to go 'round again.

And, yes, I have accumulated a wagon load of detractors, among them the Baptists of Waco and Baylor University.

(Listens to reporter)

Yes, Sir, the Baptists and I are quarreling. The papers were full of it last fall. Perhaps a schoolboy should be employed to read your own front page to you.

In these six months past, the Baptists have imposed an odious and ominous circumstance on me and my family. My wife is frightened, and my children. I have been beaten. And my friends have suffered, physically and emotionally. This town has splintered itself over my confrontation with the Baptists, but as with Shakespeare's disputatious MacBeth, "I am in blood Stepp'd in so far that, should I wade no more, Returning would be as tedious as go o'er . . ."

Last November, when the inmates of the Baylor Baptist incubator beat me and attempted to sling a number four hemp rope about my neck, I considered their intent, at the very least, unsociable. You are perhaps more knowledgeable on these matters than I, Sir, but my understanding is that lynching has not yet become an article of the Christian doctrine. 'Twas my error. Beaten, I practiced a basic tenet of

Christianity and turned the other cheek to the smackers . . . and got it smuck.

Since arrived in Waco hardly four years ago, I have seized the opportunity to study our local Baptists and, in aggregate, find them engrossing creatures.

The Bible tells us that God made a perfect man, and let him degenerate until he began breeding Baptists. A Baptist don't want to think. He just wants to believe . . . and take a bath. If he should think, he couldn't believe, and if he didn't believe, he'd be damned.

There is about the Baptists a sullen mustiness, as though merriment is a mortal sin, laughter a holy impurity. They refrain from harmless and healthful amusements in fear of displeasing their Deity. The idea appears to be that by making themselves and everybody else unnecessarily miserable in this world, their ecstasy will be enhanced in the Great Hereafter.

Their chronic gloom permeates Waco like swamp gas. And, Sir, that is an aggravation to those of us who wish to pass through this uncertain life with some fractional morsel of cheer.

They are a narrow and closed sect. When our Waco Baptists arrive in Heaven, they will, no doubt, refuse to associate with Jesus Christ because he was a carpenter, and turn up their patrician snouts at Almighty God for having worked in mud.

Being, however, an optimistic sinner, I often have my doubts about their common unhappiness, suspect that our scowling, sanctimonious Baptists are much like alley cats. You know they are out there somewhere, raising hell . . . you just can't catch 'em at it.

They are liars, Sir, though that should surprise no one. Liars are boundless in our age. People have become such incorrigible liars that I've about quit trying to borrow money. I have experienced lies and liars but I do not feel altogether qualified to write a manual on the art of lying, albeit I was for some time editor of the *San Antonio Express.*

(Listens to reporter)

What's that? Speak up! No, by God, I am not slandering newspapers. I'm a product of newspapers, as are you.

O dammit!

Sir, you are proof that nature plays no favorites. When she gives a man a lower-case brain, she makes amends by supplying him with a display-type mouth.

Slander newspapers? How is that possible?

There was a time when the principal business of the American press was the publication of important news. But it has, for the most part, dropped its high pretensions and is now notoriously out for the stuff.

Papers seem to be striving to outdo each other in journalistic idiocy. They now have taken to color illustrations and resemble nothing so much as painted bladders blown to the bursting point. Such as the *Fort Worth Register* and the *Dallas Herald,* which can spoil more white paper with vacuous prattle than any publications on Earth . . . with the possible exception of the *Houston Post.* The *Post* boasts of a tremendous circulation and I can easily believe it when I consider the large population of our lunatic asylums.

The *Austin Statesman* is a paper with no valid excuse for existing. Reading it for news were like seining the Atlantic Ocean for a bullfrog.

I will wager the *Galveston News* five hundred dollars, in gold, it cannot demonstrate it has printed, as editorial, one original idea during the past sixty days. I haven't read the paper closely, but I know its editor. The mother of that mental abnormality expends much time scratching fleas with her hind feet.

As the organ of Texas Populists, the *Southern Mercury* of Dallas easily could succeed if it had an editor, instead of an ignorant animal who thinks with his abdomen, writes with his feet, and employs his large porous ears for blotting pads.

(Pause, muses)

No, I don't believe it is possible to slander newspapers.

(Points to reporter)

Sir? Yes, you. Which of our noble Texas Dailies do you represent?

(Listens)

Ah, the *Dallas News* . . . *O tempora* . . . *O mores* . . .

(In disgusted voice)

. . . O Hell!

The Dallas News! The Old Lady of Texas Journalism. She whimpers and whines, twists and tergiversates. The editorial page of the *Dallas News* reminds me of the desert of Sahara after a simoon. It is such an awful waste of space. Her editorials resound like a muley cow pulling all four feet out of a Waxahachie mudhole.

I do not know what others may think of this but if I had a dog degraded enough to utilize a copy of the *Dallas News* as a urinal, I'd shoot him!

(Muses)

Some of these days my Christian fortitude will slip a cog or sprain a kidney and I'll say something I'll be sorry for.

I don't mean to neglect the religious press, that journalistic purgatory of my Christian colleagues.

I saw an item . . .

(Searches desk clutter for paper, finds, reads)

"The Methodist Episcopal Conference, recently assembled in New York, rejected a candidate for clerical honors because he was cross-eyed."

Wonderful! The Apostle is inclined to agree. The Methodist ministry is no place for a preacher who can look two ways at once.

I am this very week drafting a gentle rebuke to my neighbor in the next office, the Reverend J. B. Cranfill, who is, as you know, editor of the flatulent *Baptist Standard.*

The other day I passed a moment with Mr. Cranfill in our mutual building, and he asked, "Brann, are you a Christian?" I answered: "Naw . . . thank God I'm only a newspaperman."

He, being a Baptist minister, didn't find that amusing. I wonder how he will accept this:

(Searches for paper, reads)

"To the faithful in Texas, Greetings! The Apostle is deeply grieved to note there has grown up among Ye a disregard for the social decencies of true Christianity. Verily I say unto you, that 'tis useless to polish the outside of your tin platter and set it in the world's show-window unless you give the inside a swipe."

What lies heaviest on my heart is the fact that the *Standard* is in the habit of ladling out saving grace with one hand while raking in the shekels with the other for flaming advertisements of syphilitic nostrums, lost manhood restorers, and kindred quack remedies for diseases with which the faithful are supposed to be unfamiliar.

It pains me to note that the purveyors of panaceas for private diseases regard the *Baptist Standard* as the best possible medium of reaching prospective patrons.

It doth grieve the Apostle sore to see flaunted in the middle of a page of jejune babble anent the Holy Spirit a big display ad for the . . . French Nerve Pill . . . guaranteed to restallion old studs! Perhaps the Apostle is entirely too sensitive where the reputation of his Brethren in Christ is concerned but it does grate upon my nerves to see a really good sermon flanked by an advertisement of Pennyroyal Pills . . . especially designed to produce abortions!

We should ever bear in mind that while in this world we are not of it, and must be willing to subsist on corn bread and buttermilk on Earth, that we may have pie and pound cake in the Hereafter.

(Picks up copy of Baptist Standard, *scans it)*

We should not attempt to straddle the game, to serve two masters thusly:

(Reads in alternating voices)

"Remember the Sabbath Day and Keep It Holy!"
(Ladies, Pennyroyal Pills Are Safe and Sure!)
"Wine is a Mocker and Strong Drink Is Raging!"
(Victims of the Secret Vice Should Try In-da-po!)
"Believe and Be Baptized and Ye Shall Be Saved!"
(Big G Positively Cures the Worst Cases of Sexual . . . Solitaire!)

Brother Cranfill, if you persist in prostituting your columns in this manner, you will assuredly drive me out of the ministry.

O dammit!

It is entirely possible we are not holding our Baptists under water long enough!

If Cranfill and his stale *Baptist Standard* would produce even one paragraph of real Christianity, I'd do something desperate . . . I'd subscribe!

It is useless to rant on anent the *Texas Baptist Standard,* and I am weary to my soul of Cranfill's shenanigans, having all I can do to keep my own flock of webfeet Baptists paddling against the current. Let us move on. . . .

(Listens to reporter)

Politics! Of course, you would suggest politics, Sir, being, I believe, a beast of burden for the *Houston Post.* The *Post* is an incarnation of infamy, yet its editor, I am told, aspires to the lieutenant governorship of Texas. While it is true the American people have a weakness for humbugs, we cannot, by ignorance, transform a porker into a philosopher by calling it Plato, nor make a statesman of a tub of lard by electing it Lieutenant Governor.

Before pining for public office, the *Post*'s editor should get on the downwind side of himself and make a cautious inspection of his underwear.

Verily, he's got his gall, but gall is the proprietorship of each hopeful politician. They all seek a public office of low salary and high stealage.

(To reporter)

What, Sir? You are not taking notes with which to regale your political-minded editor? Probably the *Post*'s editor would not comprehend. When gawdalmighty shapes a man's head like a bedpan we can hardly expect it to hold much that's valuable.

Politics is an eccentric occupation. Has it occurred to you that the average Congressman costs this country some fifteen thousand dollars per annum, exclusive of the incidental damage he does? It is common cant that "the people make the laws." They don't. The lawyer-politicians make them, and with the full understanding that the more intricate the legal machinery may be, the more need of experts, the fatter the harvest of fees.

O dammit!

And we shall be so inflicted as long as we employ cheap labor to make our laws.

Perhaps politicians take their gall from the general public, which is in ravished clamor to nourish itself at the trough of government welfare, hangs onto the public tit like a kid-goat in a sand-blizzard. When a man lacks sufficient judgment to manage a mule and cannot be trusted in a cotton patch without a keeper, he secures a situation in the Postal Service.

The government now is looking to supervise our rail system and should it assume control of the trains and manage them as it does the paper mail, the engines would wander off into the woods. It would be necessary to send out tracers to discover the whereabouts of lost depots.

One great trouble with our government is that it is becoming too complex, too redundant. There is danger of its breaking down with its own weight. We're governed entirely too much. About every fifth man you meet is a public servant of some sort, and you cannot get married or buried, own a dog, brew a bucket of beer, shout Hallelujah, purchase a pound of putty, or get a shirt laundered except with a by-your-leave to an all-pervading law of the land.

The longer I live the more I realize that men are but children who have had the mumps.

(Checks time)

Such talk makes me thirsty. Any talk makes me thirsty. Except on Sunday. In Texas, on Sunday, a man is exempt from thirst by legislative decree. By mandated statute, it is a misdemeanor punishable by fine to labor, sell goods, or open a place of amusement on the Lord's Day. No one is permitted to do business but the hired preachers and licensed prostitutes.

Our Texas Sunday law is enforced hit and miss . . . but it is a solid bullseye in Waco.

(In sad, mournful voice)

Sunday's a dull day here.

Well, it not being Sunday, and we may legally purchase a popcorn ball and a pop, I will retire soon to George Laneri's Saloon across the street. You men may as well come along, for when the Sunday sermons are not in session, Waco's saloons are a veritable Niagara of Anheuser-Busch.

And we should hurry while Laneri's is still in the beer business. Brother Cranfill is working up a boycott against our saloons, indeed, is calling for a boycott of any merchant who is a known drinker. He and other preachers are, in fact, asking Baptists to drop the black bean on all tradesmen who do not belong to their interesting denomination.

Imagine! To succeed, the boycott would have to spread. A Baptist dry-goods dealer could not buy cloth from a Methodist mill, nor the Presbyterian green-grocer get his supplies from an Episcopalian gardener. Consider the required signs on Main Street: "Baptist Butter!" "Methodist Cornmeal!" "Cambellite Codfish!" . . . "Episcopalian Prunes!"

(Muses)

As a crusader, the Reverend Mr. Cranfill is a dismal failure, but he would be a dazzling success as ballast for a canal boat.

So we should hurry while there's still something to drink besides smokehouse kerosene and the Sassafras Tea served by Old Maids. Though there may be little anymore in that Old Maid tea legend. Times are changing. Cleopatra drank pearls dissolved in wine, but whiskey straight is said to be good enough for some of her successors.

This is the Age of the New Woman!

She is stepping out briskly, extolling her renovated freedom, even clamoring to enter the voting box. The New Woman is certainly getting there. Already she can sit cross-legged and cuss. Her costume is mannish, she can swallow four fingers of red-eye licker without blinking, has taken to real tobacco cigarettes, expects soon to be able to expectorate without craning her neck, and to scratch a match on the seat of her pants.

(Listens to reporter)

Oh? A slander of women, you say? No Sir, I do not defame them. I married one and must return home now and again.

The Iconoclast is distinctly the ladies' paper. It believes in the superiority of the sex. It is in favor of giving woman not only everything she wants, but everything she thinks she wants. Give her the ballot . . . and the box; the Earth and the fullness thereof. Give her the moon for a parasol and the stars where-with to bedeck her bodice and emblazon her garters . . . then give her me. Let her enjoy all the rights, privileges, and prerogatives of the proudest American citizens that wear "pants." Let her parade in torch light procession, exhibit her best bonnet on the hustings, run for office and buy votes in blocks of five. She could scarce make a worse mess of representative government than have the men.

I do, however, admit a hillock of curiosity about this burgeoning female revolution, as many young ladies rush into literature instead of the laundry, become poets of passion instead of authors of pie. Women are beginning to indulge in what once was the sole property of men: Humbuggery. I am told that many ladies now wear patent complexions, store-bought bangs, and pad out their scrawny forms until they appear voluptuous Junos, thereby to deceive and beguile.

Much of this deceit, however, occurs within our Social Set. A Vanderbilt daughter recently ensnared one of those macaroni princes common to the waste dumps of Europe. She found her prince on the matrimonial bargain-counter and gathered him in . . . paid for him, much as one might purchase a hairless Mexican pup.

This gangle-shanked, putty-faced girl is, as they say, big for her size. Her horizontal having developed at the expense of her perpendicular, Miss Vanderbilt's beauty is that voluptuous type know to the Euphuists as Junoesque, but called by the Common Herd, Oleomargaramic.

She dressed for the wedding in a skillion dollars worth of finery, including a bonnet of songbird feathers. Such a woman who will sacrifice a songbird on the altar of her vanity would embalm her baby and wear it as a brooch if Dame Fashion decreed it. A wise husband would hesitate to insure his life in favor of such a creature, for she'd pour hot lead in his ear or dope his dinner to secure the price of a new dress.

(Listens to reporter)

Yes, yes . . . I will treat this matter with more gravity.

When I reflect that until comparatively recent times, women were slaves, I don't wonder that the old civilizations went to the dogs. For ages, woman was but man's plaything, valuable chiefly for breeding purposes. The highest educational advantages were denied her, the professions closed against her as an incapable. Her talents were supposed to be small, and little opportunity was offered for their enlargement.

But the world is growing wiser, and woman is pressing eagerly forward into the widening field.

The New Woman simply is a hard-sensed young lady who politely, but pointedly, declines to play second fiddle in the great diapason of humanity, refuses to be bound by inept customs that have cursed her sex for sixty centuries. She does not object to matrimony but declines to regard the capture of some sapheaded dude with a few dollars as the end and aim or her existence. She prefers to gird up her patent health corset and go out into the world to settle her own hash.

It is not true, has never been true, as is perpetuated by the religious hoo-doos and whang-doodles that woman introduced snake-sin to the world and thereby is eternally damned. Women fill our churches. . . . I sometime believe that Heaven will be populated only by women, with just enough men in residence to fill the municipal offices. Women are in church to receive God's blessings, which they richly deserve.

Whatever may have been Eve's fortune, Adam was no great loser by being ejected from Eden, for the man who possesses the love of a good woman carries Paradise with him wherever he goes.

(Listens to reporter)

Your question, Sir: Would I allow my wife to be a New Woman?

(Bemused pause)

You are a bachelor, are you not?

My wife has not yet informed me what she will allow me to allow her to become.

O dammit!

(Listens to reporter)

No, Sir, it is not unseemly for a lady to . . . hustle her own hash. To advance one's self is not, as you suggest, unladylike. It is human.

(Listens to reporter)

Inez . . . my daughter? She is dead. . . . No, you did not know. It . . . was long ago.

(Long pause)

I wrote of it, of her death . . . and sealed away my words . . .

(Pause)

. . . she died a long time ago . . . but always, she is in my mind.

(Pause)

She was small . . . with brown, bright eyes, and gentle with all who knew her. She met everyone with a smile and generous words. Inez was beautiful.

When scarce passed to her 'teens, the youthful swains began to sigh for her, to bring flowers to our door. One was of her own age, and he haunted our street until I noticed him. I spoke harshly, sharply, to Inez: "You encourage the little fool! Speak to him no more!"

She replied: "But, Father, I never spoke to him, nor he to me."

She arose, went into the street, and the boy followed. I was enraged, believing she had lied.

"Inez, you have deceived me!"

". . . O, Father!"

At home, she sat in silence, brooding on the great wrong. Her eyes filled with tears that seemed frozen by pride. They never fell. The gust of my anger, my breath of doubt, made her world desolate. I kissed her goodnight but she did not respond.

While I slept, she wrote, in her precise hand, a letter. The words burn and reverberate in my memory still:

(Recites, in monotone)

"Tomorrow I will be dead. I took all the morphine. I don't want to live. I could never be as good as you want me to. You would be ashamed of me. I hope God will take me to Heaven."

(Pause)

I kissed her dead lips and buried my precious Inez but not my shame. God knows, as I know: I killed her. I killed my own daughter with a father's anger and blindness.

She was thirteen.

Would I care if my daughter were . . . A New Woman? Great God in Heaven, man, I would care neither that she was a New Woman, nor an old. I would care that she be all that she could be. I would care nothing but that she be happy.

O dammit!

The most perfect life is not worth the living for itself alone. There's still more shadow than sunshine, less pleasure than pain. We struggle valiantly . . . for what? All life is but a dream and we know not when we sleep nor when we wake. We waste our lives enacting a foolish farce and vainly trying to make the world believe it is a reality.

We are fools, you and I. We feast on Hope that our pain of life is but temporary. We ache with our days and nights that we might feel peace in the Eternity. I hope . . . because I must. Without Hope, my pain is too much. My ignorance and anger killed Inez. My Hope keeps me alive, as your Hope sustains you.

We will, I believe, survive this rag-tag, gossamer existence . . . because we must. God forgive us!

(Pause, in a more optimistic voice)

And He will forgive us . . . for the Almighty, fortunately, deals in damaged goods.

So come, let us relax for awhile. I have need of the warm companionship of such a place as Laneri's.

No doubt we will see several of my Baptist friends there, pretending they are not drinking beer in public. A saloon is like that. It brings together the dissidents of this sinful world, a fact that possibly fulfills Biblical prophesy. The Good Book tells us that in our age the lion shall lie down with the lamb.

Perhaps that shall come to pass . . . but the lamb will sleep with one foot on the floor.

(Exits)

CURTAIN

Act Two

(In an expansive, jovial mood, Brann enters, moves downstage, speaks:)

What a glorious spring! The flowers would shame a rainbow. They emit a rare airy perfume. The breezes are breezing. The sun is sunning. Our Earth is renewing itself once again, and all's right in God's world, even Waco, which is, as you know, His root cellar.

I apologize for my tardy return but the brew was cold, the saloon warm with laughter and conviviality, and the conversation heady and awash with gossip of the best type: salacious and unproven.

My colleagues of the press . . .

(Looks for reporters)

. . . I see you have returned in a somewhat sober, if intellectually depleted, condition. My colleagues and I elevated our glasses in declarations of mutual admiration and filled the spring-cleansed air with debate, during which we actually discovered an area of agreement: We are against the rising specter of Prohibitionism!

When, in that happier world beyond the skies, we are permitted to praise God without pausing for meals, we will probably learn why He elected to plague this Earth with thorns and thistles, pismires and Prohibitionists. The Prohibs would isolate us by water, and indeed, water is an indispensable. But too much of it once wrecked the world. It is common knowledge that the Lord kept that old sot, Noah, for seed, while letting the Prohibitionists drown.

They probably mean well but the Prohibs are incapable of learning that so long as whiskey is made it will be drunk, that Prohibitionism means simply a poorer brand of booze. The Prohibs claim the Bible supports their position. A lie.

The Bible in no way comes out for Prohibition . . . but it does make circumcision obligatory.

A law to stop drinking? Such gibberish curdles my cocktail!

Go ahead, thou sanctimonious slang-slingers! Make Waco a dry town. Compel us to import our beer and ice it at home. The bottles will make handy playthings for the babies. Waco will then be a nice quiet resort for overworked people from Dallas and Fort Worth when they want complete rest, and the grass in our streets will make a charming refuge for the mule-eared rabbit.

The Prohibs should put the question to the voters.

We in the saloon took a poll on Prohibition. To a man, we were against it!

The People Have Spoken!

We were in agreement about whiskey, but we engaged, with mixed results, in a lively discussion on the true Christian merits of my old adversary, T. DeWitt Talmage.

Reverend Talmage is in his dream period, nightly transporting himself around Heaven to inspect what God hath fashioned. Like a Persian Dervish, he can, by gazing steadfastly into his own chimeran umbilicus, see wondrous things to come.

What strikes me curious is how Brother Talmage can mail a copy of his Sunday sermon out on Wednesday, disclosing a dream he is to have in sleep on Saturday. Now, that is a miracle!

Of late, he has been giving his version of Heaven, tossing in *The Iconoclast*'s name now and then for spice and countermelody, detailing how I am a consistent critic of God. Of course, every man's an Atheist who doesn't see God through Talmage's telescope. He assumes a criticism of himself is an insult to the Creator.

Noting the superiority of Talmage asleep to Talmage awake leads me to wonder what kind of iridescent genius he'll be when he's dead.

In all his stertorous pilgrimages, he has never discovered the inhabitants doing aught in which a man of sense could take the slightest interest. They appear always to be glorifying . . . throwing bouquets at Father, Son, and Holy Ghost. I cannot imagine the Trinity finding satisfaction in the eternal soft soap of a gang of triflers who escaped hell only by the skin of their teeth. Think of the Creator of the

Cosmos being tickled throughout all Eternity by the cringing adulation of a Talmage, by millions of slaves ever circling 'round his throne and crying "Holy! Holy! Holy!" and charivariing Him with cymbals, harps, and horns! Perhaps Brother Talmage could be happy in such a place but me . . . I'd . . . I'd raise hell!

(Pause)

Lord, how that man dreams!

Well, I can dream, too. I suffered with one last evening. I dreamed that a school of mosquito wiggle-tails in a barrel of rainwater under my window were discussing me. They had a tradition that I built the barrel for their special benefit, and believed that they'd eventually grow wings and go to me. Most of them did.

One smart young wiggler, evidently just from college, ridiculed the tradition and denied my existence. He wanted to know: If I made the barrel . . . who made me?

His brethren undertook to argue with him, but as he easily bested them, they concluded that he was guilty of blasphemy and that it was their Christian duty to beat the head off him. As they were leading him to execution, I leaned out of my window.

(Speaks in alternating voices)

"Here!" I demanded. "What are you vermin doing?"

"Good Sir," answered an old patriarch. "This wicked young wiggler denies your existence."

"Well, what of it? I'm here just the same!"

"But he takes your name in vain!"

"Have you noticed me missing any meals on that account? Suppose I lie awake to sob because a dodgasted little wiggle-tail rears up and makes free with my name?"

"But he reviles our holy priesthood and ridicules our religion!"

"I thought so! You denounce him, not that he's doing me any harm but because he has wounded *your* vanity by questioning *your* wisdom. You think you're o'erflowing with grace when you're only filled to the nozzle with gall. Now, you subside and attend strictly to your own business. . . . or I'll break your barrel!"

I've looked through all the dream books to learn what this remarkable vision may mean, but without avail. Perhaps, like the dreams of Talmage, it simply signifies that I absorbed too much boned turkey and slept on my back.

(Listens to reporter)

I quarrel with your charge. I am no heretic. A heretic, my sententious Sir, is a fellow who disagrees with you regarding something which neither of you know anything about.

(Listens to reporter)

No, by God, Talmage's dream was not a celestial vision! He knows no more of Heaven than a gotch-eyed dog. Neither do I. Nor you. None does.

How can we? We are limited by our imagination. Our highest possible conception of Heaven is but the world we know made perfect. We cannot so much think of it except by the aid of Earthly symbols. It is an idealization of the real, an intensification of what we find best in this life, most beautiful. Our Heaven is what we wish life could be.

And, our Hell is the reality of man's worst fears.

I believe I am more confident of Hell than Heaven. I have already experienced its ravaging heat, having lived two years in Houston.

No doubt sixty thousand Americans go to Hell every year, and quite deservedly, too, for that many Republicans die.

(Pause)

At the saloon, we lifted our glasses in tribute to my friend here.

(Indicates a reporter)

He is to be married soon and felt the need for strong, steadying drink. And well he should. Marriage, I submit, is perhaps the only game of chance ever invented at which it is possible for both players to lose.

I know all about love, but what it truly is, I am not prepared to say. It comes upon us at uncertain times, like the mumps, and raises welts on our hearts, beats the be-jams out of our heads, flails away at our senses with the beatific enthusiasm of a still-damp Baptist.

Love is the law of life, the breath of which the Universe was born, but love is like all other sweet things. Unless you get the very best brand, it sours awful easy. Like seasickness, everybody laughs at love but the fellow who's got it.

It is . . . O dammit! . . . it's that which transforms a snub-nosed dairy maid into a Grecian goddess, a bench-legged farmer boy into a living Apollo. I have explained love often, even debated with a subscriber over in England whether love is intoxicating. I suspect it is, though I could not undertake scientific experiments to prove my thesis. Suppose I had done so, found that love makes citizens drunk, and was run in by the patrol wagon while supercharged with tender passion? Don't you see that would militate against my usefulness as a Baptist minister? How the hell could I explain to my congregation that I was full of love instead of licker?

I do know there is none immune to romance, and the best of us will sometime nibble at love's hook when baited with a sunbonnet and a pair of bloomers, or a promised kiss.

When I love a woman, I love her up one side and down t'other. I may be an uncultured and barbaric noodle, but I want to get hold of her and bite her neck. I believe with Tennyson in the "spirits rushing together at the touching of the lips," and I just let 'em rush.

Kissing, though, is becoming a risky pastime. Some little smart-aleck doctor has mounted his pulpit to inform a foolish world that kissing is dangerous, that the roseate lips of beauty are a skull and crossbones crammed to the cranium with disease germs.

It is well-known, however, that doctors are somewhat addicted to failure. Consider the fact that when they began writing their prescriptions in Latin, it quickly became a dead language.

This doctor opines that all danger may be avoided if the kissing couple is carefully deodorized before and after use, recommends that lips be washed with some chemical compound. It's a great scheme but it won't work here. In Texas, a man must take his kiss with the peeling on, or go without.

It might have profit in Chicago, perhaps, for the Yankee Midwest has fallen into the bad habit of promiscuous kissing, a social rite as stale and flat as employing a community toothbrush or an indiscriminate swapping of gum.

O dammit!

Once I attended a church fair in Missouri and found two local beauties of a good family retailing kisses to all comers for two bits apiece. It was for the Lord's work in the missionary field, they said.

I bought five dollars of the sweetness . . . then hired as my surrogate smoocher an old farmer who enjoyed a bad case of catarrh and had worn his solitary tooth down to the Pliocene period chewing plug tobacco.

The girls suddenly lost interest in helping the foreign mission gang. It was the Lord's loss but, then, the Lord didn't have to kiss that toothless old farmer!

Disease germs, indeed! Kiss away, my friends, kiss away. This sinful old world can absorb more love than it now has on hand.

(Listens to reporter)

No, Sir, I am not against Christian charity.

But Christian charity is not peddling kisses for a quarter a smack, nor small children's pennies collected for the benefit of transforming Buddhists into Baptists.

You people who have prayers and Bible readings before breakfast while your hearts vibrate between holiness and hash, between Christ and the cook, should recognize Christian charity, but it's dollars to doughnuts you don't.

It is toleration, it is kindness, it is humanity, it is Truth. It is the Spirit of God made manifest in Man. Christian charity is human tolerance, a commodity I find in scarce supply as we near the twentieth century of current human history.

Look at your front pages, Gentlemen. The Christian world today points a finger of scorn at Islams for evangelizing with the Koran in one hand and a scourge in the other. I have not taken the Moslem under my apostolic protectorate, but it is not necessary to go back far to find American religious atrocities in, as one example, Massachusetts, where blessed Christians tortured their neighbors as witches and, with red-hot irons, bored the tongues of Quakers.

The Jew has been regarded with suspicion by Christians for a score of centuries, though our ancestors were but brutal barbarians clad in skins from beasts when the Jews were framing those laws which are the basic principles of civilization. Jews wove into the woof of human history those imperishable gems of philosophy which the world's wisest say transcend the genius of man and must be the gracious gift of God.

Yet, there are some Christians today who seriously debate whether the Jew has a soul!

American Catholics, who are among our most law-abiding citizens, are charged by deluded Christians as anarchists who would install their Pope as ruler of these United States.

Sir, I have heard our Waco churchmen complain harshly of the foreign savage, then collect loose coins with which to herd those poor creatures into Christian corrals, but would not welcome them into the five thousand-dollar churches built here in America while children are begging bread and women are dying of want and men are glad to work three times a week for a dollar a day!

What this world needs is more broad-guage Christianity and less hidebound dogmatism, more substance and less ceremony, more hard hustling and less harping at the Lord for help.

(Listens to reporter)

Mock religion? I mock nothing that raises man.

I admit I do not believe the snake story. I object to being dressed in feathers after death and having to work overtime hymning and hosannah-ing. I give up nary a nickel to send fat missionaries to hungry heathen. But perhaps the unkindest thing yet said of me is that I mock and wage war on religion.

I do not!

I would not for the life of me insult and belittle those sincere Christians who believe even the Bible's very chapter headings to have been handwritten by God.

I am not warring upon religious faith but on those pulpit-thrumming gowkthrapples who peddle hallelujahs at two dollars apiece and mistake bile for benevolence, gall for Godliness, and chronic laziness for a "call to preach," those who fail the supreme test of a charitable mind . . . toleration for the opinions of others, the admission that perchance we do not know it quite all.

My only quarrel is with the ministry. Too many of its members are unworthy of their high calling, are too much given to dogmatizing about the Deity instead of teaching the religion of Brotherly Love. There are a great many grand and noble ministers, but there also are too many hacking 'round with their little hoes in the Lord's Vineyard who would do more effective work in the cotton patch . . . or the penitentiary.

They forget, my friend, that God is everywhere . . . even in church.

Too many lack Christian tolerance, and my little broad-bladed sword is out for them. You can't reform society from the bottom, you must begin at the top.

There are ministers who are so cold to human charity and tolerance that their children are born with frost on them.

I have written to them . . .

(Searches for paper, reads)

"You may yawp in your pulpit until ice forms in perdition, and agonize in prayer until your collar limps and you break a lung. You may paddle about in your baptismal tank until you develop dorsal fins and web feet. You may believe the Bible from Alpha to Omega and the Baptist credo from A to Izzard . . . but if you have not true Christian charity, you are no more than a cracked cymbal at a ten-cent circus."

Such men do not live. They merely exist. They do not enjoy life. They do not even suffer its pangs, know naught of its sweetness.

God pity them!

(Listens to reporter)

No, I do not exempt Baptists from God's pity, but who began this thing? Before *The Iconoclast* was three days old, it was boycotted by that hydrocephalous sect.

Remember last fall, just six months ago when this bloody sorrow began, they brought the ex-priest Slattery to Waco, to lie about American Catholics, and worse, to declare the pious nuns prostitutes. Slattery's last harangue was delivered to men only and the house was packed with Baptists and Baylorites at four bits a head. The so-called lecture was the foulest thing that ever fell from the lips of mortal man, yet the Baptist audience gloated over it.

Unable to restrain my indignation, I arose and denounced every utterance a malicious lie. Immediately the audience cried, "Throw him out! Down with him!" I chanced to have my back near the side wall, that's why I was not mobbed.

No, I didn't start this thing, though I intend to finish it, if it does not first finish me. I could not tolerate Slattery's lies. Our Catholics are not subversive agents of the Pope intent on enslaving America, nor are their convents harems for priests! Such putrid falsehoods must be answered!

Hardly had Slattery removed his 250 stall-fed pounds from Waco when we learned the plight of little Antonia Teixeira.

How could any man ignore such a damnable crime? Have you heard her tragic story, Sir? Have you? I did what I could to ensure that the world knew of poor, sad Antonia.

Missionaries snatched her from Brazil, from Catholicism, a veritable brand from the burning, and promised her widowed mother she would be given five years' schooling at Baylor University, then returned home a cultured, educated lady to give witness to others of the wondrous ways of Baptists.

Hardly eleven years old, she was brought to Waco, was consecrated, and began her studies at Baylor . . . not in the classroom, as promised before God, but in the kitchen of Dr. Burleson, Baylor's president.

Instead of digging Greek roots, she was studying the succulent potato peel, slinging hash instead of mastering Hebrew. Perhaps the poor girl thought that scrubbing floors was part of a liberal education.

After some three years of the kitchen curricula, she was examined and it was found that she had not made much progress toward effective missionary work. Oh, she had heard something of the Protestant faith and salvation by water, but more dusting and dishwashing were necessary before being ready to preach the gospel. She was returned to the kitchen.

Then, suddenly, it was discovered this little ward of Baylor was about to give birth!

Thus her dishrag and scrub broom studies were suspended and she was spirited away to a private home.

Dr. Burleson never concerned himself with her plight . . . until secular law officials learned of the tragedy. She told them how she had been drugged and dragged from her culinary classroom and three times criminally assaulted . . . by the brother of Dr. Burleson's son-in-law!

A medical examination demonstrated conclusively the physical outrage and lacerations she suffered.

And what was Dr. Burleson's response to this criminal attack of a child under his protection? He rushed into print with a statement that Antonia was a thief and crazy after the boys! His son-in-law, a Baptist minister, charged that the father of her unborn child was a Negro servant!

Ye Gods! Ye Gods! Ye pitying Gods!

And Antonia no older than my precious Inez!

It was at that point I sharpened up my little copy pencil and leapt into the Baptists with words a-flying!

Finally, and prematurely, Antonia gave birth . . . a pretty two-pound Baylor diploma. It was white.

But, sadly, the child died. Today, Antonia is gone from Waco, safe from the Baptists, her accused attacker secure from prosecution. Antonia's tragedy has divided Waco, and I have more holes in my head than nature intended because Baylor took offense that I would inform the world about its criminal treatment of little girls.

(Listens to reporter)

Yes, I attacked Baylor, because it attacked me. I do not consider it indispensable to Waco.

You heard the rumor in the saloon, Sir? That Dallas wants Baylor? Doubtless, I'm a hopeless heretic but I don't believe a damn word of it. Dallas doesn't want Baylor, even a little bit. There isn't a town in the world that wants it, except . . . Wack-o.

It is simply another Frankenstein monster that has destroyed its architect. Its students chiefly are forks-of-the-road yaps who curry horses and run errands for their board and wear the same undershirt year-round.

The institution is worth less than nothing to any town. It is the Alma Mater of mob violence, a chronic breeder of bigotry and bile, and as a small Waco property owner, I will give it one thousand dollars any time to move to Dallas, and double that amount if it will go to Honolulu.

(Pause, softer)

In reality, I have no consequential quarrel with the school. *The Iconoclast* would like to see Baylor University, so called, become an honor to Texas instead of an educational eyesore, would like to hear it spoken of with reverence instead of sneering. I desire to see Baylor a veritable Pantechnicon of learning, at least a place where the careful student may acquire something really worth remembering, instead of being a mere Squeeritic graft to relieve simple Baptist folk of their hard-earned boodle by befuddling the brains of their children with miscalled education.

The faculty of Baylor is composed of superficially educated instructors who know even less than is contained in the textbooks. People cannot impart information which they do not possess.

Hence, the graduates of Baylor have not been really educated but rather what the erstwhile Mr. Shakespeare would call . . . clapper-clawed.

To run a genius through Baylor would be like running an eagle through a thrashing machine. It would require years for him to recover.

I would not destroy Baylor. I would make it better. I would deprive the ignorant and vicious of control. I would expel all the hoodlums whose brutality and cowardice have disgraced it. I would make its diplomas badges of honor, as in the old days, instead of certificates of illiteracy at which public school children laugh.

Change is the order of the Universe, and as Baylor cannot very well become worse, it must of necessity become better. It has my unswerving support. I am even willing to conduct a night school free of charge for instruction of its faculty if each member thereof will give bond not to seek a better-paying situation as soon as he learns something.

(Listens to reporter)

I understand, and share your concern, Sir. Yes, this town is rent with rage and sadness, and all of us must share the blame.

I intend to write nothing more, and am about done dallying with the Baptist faith. Enough is plenty. I leave in the morning on an extended lecture tour and perhaps by the time I return the Baptists will have learned some common sense.

(Listens to reporter)

No! No, by God!

The Baptists are not running me out of town!

They have tried that, and failed. I do not run, Sir, from cowards, especially those who send young boys and beginning Baptists to fight for them.

No, I do not run, even though Baylor's Biblical scholars return again with their ropes and threats. I have no revenge to gratify. If Socrates were poisoned by the splenetic-hearted hypocrites of his time, it would ill become me to complain of a milder martyrdom for a like offense.

Because of them, the Baylor students, I enjoyed my first vacation in fifteen years. I devoted the major part of a month last Autumn digesting the Saving Grace administered by my Baptist Brethren. Their sermon was rubbed in with revolvers and ropes, loaded canes and miscellaneous cudgels. My Baptist friends desired to send me as a missionary to foreign lands, and their invitation was so urgent, I wore my head in a sling and had to write with my left hand.

In the Fall, after my articles about Antonia, Baylor University . . . that little museum of mental misfits . . . became an armed camp with squads of students patrolling at night. And the grown-up Baptists met and howled they were "willing to sign Brann's death-warrant" for what they believed was my intolerable treatment of the school.

Naturally, the students, not being blessed with brains, came for my hide. They found me in my office, from which they dragged me to the campus, beat me, threatened to lynch me from the branches of that venerable oak before Old Main . . . as faculty members stood and wrung their hands.

I escaped, and a week later the Baptists were at me again. A mob of men battered me with six-shooters and bludgeons until I was insensible. I can overlook the assault of the students, as they were encouraged by their elders, but the last attack was led by a member of the Board of Managers of Baylor!

I seek no further trouble with them. They are perfectly safe so far as I am concerned. I will go lecture and let us pray the Baptists will be serene when I return.

But if they regret they were beaten off 'ere they quite succeeded in sending me to Kingdom Come, they have only to notify me of where and when they can be found, and I'll give the whole accursed mob a show for its money. I'm too slow for a slugger, cannot lick a herd of steers with one pair of hands, but I can make a shotgun sing . . . "Come to Christ!"

I walk the streets of Waco day-by-day and I walk them alone. Let these Baptists shoot me in the back if they dare.

If the decent people of this community fail to chase them to their holes and feed their viscera to the dogs, then I'd rather be dead and in Hades forever than alive in Waco a single day!

(Listens to reporter)

O dammit!

I am sick to my soul of that lie! Does an attack on hypocrisy ever damn me to Hell?

Infidel! Heretic! Atheist!

I am none of those.

Why quarrel about our faiths and declare that this is right and that wrong, when all religions are, and must of necessity forever be, fundamentally one and the same.

Cult wars with cult and sect with sect, while all unite to damn the independent worshiper. Yet every man who bows the knee or breathes a prayer to any God of whatsoever name . . . every Egyptian bending at Isis's fanes . . . Every Phoenician sacrificing unto Baal . . . every Catholic following the Sacred Cross . . . Every Peruvian adoring the rising sun . . . every Methodist agonizing at the mourner's bench . . . all are members of the same great church.

They may worship their God in diverse ways but their faiths, when stripped of nonessentials, are one and the same. Their deities are identical.

There is a Deity. I have felt His presence. I ask no written covenant with Him. I will trust God without requiring priests and prophets to endorse His note.

Last night, as I wrote, my little son, Billy, awoke, alarmed by some noise, and came groping through the darkness to my door. He saw the light shining through the transom and returned to his trundle bed and his dreams, secure that his father was near. He knew that beyond that gleam, his father keeps watch and he asks no more.

Why should I fear the Sleep of Death? Why should I seek assurance of the Almighty's wisdom, love, and power from the lips of man . . . for through a million celestial transoms streams the Light of God.

There are great truths in the Bible. It matters not to me whether they were revealed to Hebrew prophets in delirious trance-vision or borrowed of gentile philosophers who painfully worked them out by long years of study. There they are, with the stamp of God on them. Deep pools of wisdom there are in that strange old book. Beautiful things there are, too, sometimes appearing as restful valleys amid the awful grandeur of thunder.

(Pause, softer)

I am no Atheist. I have little patience with non-believers. Why play at Atheism because others have failed to describe the indescribable, to comprehend the incomprehensible, and make it plain to men of little minds?

I met an Atheist not long ago. He was argumentative and inflexible, saying his reason accepted nothing in this world that could not be proven with absolute certainty.

I asked him: "Why then, Sir, do you take such an abiding interest in your wife's children?"

(Pause)

I should, I suppose, leave Waco for good and transfer my paper to less volatile climes. But I got together eleven thousand dollars not long ago and put it into a house. It is the first money worth talking about I ever had, and our first real home. Aside from that, a publication acquires a savor of the soil in which it springs and it is mighty risky business to try and transplant it.

I am, however, infernally tired of the wrangling it produces. I want only to write and sit in my garden to hear the mockingbirds trill the gladness of their hearts in song, and tell my children stories of elves and trolls, goblins and good spirits, and other wondrous, magical things of life.

My greatest fear is that I am a fad and may pass away when my vogue is done . . .

. . . a two-dollar rocket on a dark night. . . .

(Long pause)

I have learned something from this, this tragedy. I was taught that ours was a land of religious liberty where every man is privileged to worship God in his own way, or ignore Him altogether. And that it was my duty to insist upon this right, both for myself and for my fellows. I once entertained the idea that so long as I spoke reverently of God and respectfully of all religions, I would expose hypocrites without offending the average run of church people. I know better now. I criticized their preachers and in so doing affronted them.

And my great sadness is that not one of them has ever tried to convert me. Not one of them has ever tried, by kindly argument, to convince me I was wrong. Not one of them ever invited me to church, or so far as I can learn, prayed for me.

Perhaps they believe I am past redemption.

(Pause)

Perhaps I am. . . .

(Brann freezes as stage lights dim. Single, strong overhead spot on desk. Offstage, shots are heard. Actor speaks from darkened stage.)

"On Friday, April first, 1898, six o'clock in the evening, a block from his office in downtown Waco, William Brann was shot in the back by Tom Davis, a businessman embittered by The Iconoclast's *criticism of Baylor University. Mortally wounded, Brann turned, drew his pistol and fired four shots into Davis. Both men died within a few hours.*

"The crowd attending Brann's funeral was the largest in Waco's history. Long after his burial in Oakwood Cemetery, a monument was erected for the Iconoclast at his unmarked grave. The monument contains a bas-relief *profile of Brann. The stone has no name, no identifying legend, just the weathered profile, and a single word: Truth."*

O dammit!

(Actor, again as Brann, moves beside desk into cone of light)

The Sacred Books of all the centuries are essentially the same, the half-articulate voice of the world crying for light, the frantic efforts of Man to learn whence he came and whither he goes, to lift the veil that shrouds the two eternities . . . to see, to know.

I gather them . . . the Old Testament and the New, the Koran and the Sacred Vedas, the Northern Sagas and the Southern Mythologies. I search them through, not to scoff, but to collect, with reverent soul, every gleam of light that since the Birth of Time has vouchsafed to Man.

I read the Revelations and ponder the Prophecies.

I listen once again to the Voice in the burning bush and the mystic Whisperings of the Dodona Oak.

I descend into the Delphic Cave and stand with uncovered head to hear the voice of Memnon answer the rosy fingers of the morn.

I sit with Siddartha beneath the Bodhi tree and follow the Prophet of Islam in all his pilgrimages.

I stand with Moses on Sinai's gleaming crest and listen to the Prayer of Christ in the Garden of Gethsemane.

Then I go forth beneath the eternal stars and they seem like the eyes of pitying angels, watching Man work out little by little through the long ages, the mystery of life. . . .

(Pause)

If there is no Fatherhood of God, there can be no Brotherhood of Man.

We are one, you and I . . . bewildered, fragile, drifting, solitary, strayed, frightened, finite scraps of Eternity.

We are all one.

Do you wonder that we pray to the same God?

We must. Only a God who would tolerate me . . . would tolerate you.

(Brann freezes as lights dim)

STAGE TO BLACK

CURTAIN

Source Notes to the Lexicon

For readers fortunate enough to have access to the 12 volume bound set of *The Iconoclast* published by The Brann Publishers, Inc., New York City, 1919, the following volume and page references are provided (NA—not available).

N

O

P

Q

R

S

T

U

O dammit!

W

Epilogue

TERRIFFIC, DEADLY CONFLICT.

A Fearful Street Fight, in Which W. C. Brann and Tom E. Davis Were Riddled With Pistol Shots and Wm. H. Ward Shot Through the Hand.

BRANN, EDITOR OF ICONOCLAST, DEAD.

The Life of Tom E. Davis, the Well Known Real Estate Man of Waco, Hangs by a Thread, With Almost Every Chance Against Him.

BRANN-BAYLOR AFFAIR THE CAUSE.

A Mortoman and Musician Wounded By Flying Missiles—Ward in Jail on a Charge of Assault to Murder The City Thrown Into a Whirlwind of Excitement Over the Fearful Affair and Happy Homes Made Sad

At this writing, 9 o'clock, W. C. Brann, editor of Brann's Iconoclast, and Tom E. Davis, a prominent real estate man of this city, lie dangerously wounded with a likelihood of their dying at any moment. William H. Ward, an employe of W. C. Brann, is shot through the right hand. Sigh Kennedy, a motorman on the street car line, is shot in the right knee, and Kepler, a traveling musician, is shot in the right foot. The three men last named are only slightly wounded.

W. C. Brann is shot through the left groin, in the right foot and through the middle of the back about the lower part of the shoulder blade, ranging upward and outward, coming out at the front side near the point where the arm joins the body.

Tom E. Davis is shot twice in the right arm, the balls going through the arm, leaving four holes, once in the upper left arm near the shoulder on the outer part of the arm, the ball [illegible]

Fourth street surging around French's news stand, while there were two-thirds that number at the city hall, where Mr. Brann was being attended to, and up until after midnight the streets were filled with hundreds and hundreds of citizens grouped here and there in all the hotels, and on the street corners discussing the one absorbing question, "the shooting."

At midnight both Mr. Davis and Mr. Brann were alive, with the former resting much easier. The following is the anti-mortem statement of Mr. Davis as taken by County Clerk Joney Jones in the presence of witnesses:

"I left my office and started for Manchester's livery stable. At the corner of Franklin and Fourth streets I passed Brann and Ward. Brann remarked, there goes the damn — of a b— that has caused all my trouble. I passed on and went to Manchester's stable on some business, then came on back to Waite's saloon and stopped for a drink. I then started for my office, but near Haber's store on Bunker's alley, I met them again. They began to curse and abuse me again. [illegible] they followed [illegible] urinal in the rear, then [illegible] to the front of the [illegible] Brann said [illegible] of a b— [illegible] Brann then pulled his gun and I [illegible] at him. My arm [illegible] The reason he [illegible] loyal to [illegible] myself. [illegible] shot me after [illegible]

postoffice. Almost immediately after Brann left, Davis left me and walked up Fourth street towards his office, and I saw him cross the street to his office. I then advanced to the edge of the sidewalk and stood htre alone, I think about four or five minutes, when I heard a shot in the direction of Davis' office. I looked that way and three shots seemed to be fired almost simultaneously. Davis fell to the sidewalk and writhed as if in terrible agony. Brann seemed to be nearest to Davis, a large man being close in Brann's rear. This man I learned afterwards was W. H. Ward. While Davis was rolling on the sidewalk both of these men ran upon Davis firing very rapidly as they did so. They seemed to poke their pistols almost against Davis' body as they fired. I think fifteen or sixteen shots were fired in all. After the first four or five shots the smoke became too dense to see all that occurred. The first sight seemed to chill my blood and I became too horrified to move.

SHERMAN VAUGHN.

Sherman Vaughn said:

I was passing along Fourth street and reached a spot just in front of George Lanert's saloon. I heard a shot, and looking toward the place from whence the sound came, I saw Tom Davis reeling backward toward the wall in front of his place of business. He either fell against the sign in front of his office or the wall. I could not tell which. Mr. Brann was standing some eight or ten feet from him with a pistol in his hand, and smoke was between them. Then followed a rapid succession of shots. I could not see Mr. Davis shoot for the smoke, but could see Mr. Brann plainly. Mr. Davis fell to the sidewalk and then rose almost to his feet and fell again. He then rolled along the sidewalk toward the alley and must have turned over half a dozen times. Then another man whom I do not know joined in and he and Brann fired shot after shot at Mr. Davis as he rolled along the sidewalk. The police then came up and took Mr. Brann away. I did not see what became of the other man.

AB VAUGHAN.

Mr. Ab Vaughan [illegible]

Waco Times-Herald, April 2, 1898. Courtesy of The Texas Collection, Baylor University, Waco, Texas.